Mary Queen of Scots

A Brief History

by
Ian Douglas

Copyright

Text copyright © Ian Douglas 2018-2019

First edition published 2018

Second edition published 2019

Photographs copyright © Ian Douglas 2018-2019 unless otherwise stated.

All rights reserved. No part of this publication may be reproduced, stored in a retrieval system, or transmitted, in any form or any means, electronic, mechanical, photocopying, recording or otherwise, except as permitted by the UK Copyright, Designs and Patents Act 1988, without the prior permission in writing of the author.

Acknowledgements

I am indebted to Caroline Douglas, Chris McWhirter and Hazel Spencer for reading and making valuable comments on a draft of this book. I didn't always take their advice though, and if you identify a mistake you will have found an example.

Please see the author's website www.theheritagephotographer.com for articles on history, and particularly Scottish history

Table of Contents

Preface *6*

1. Mary's Early Years *8*
    Scotland When Mary Was Born 8
    Mary's Family and Childhood 9
    Mary's Coronation 15
    The "Rough Wooing" 17

2. Mary in France *21*

3. Religion and Politics *26*
    The Religious Divide in Scotland 26
    John Knox - a (K)noxious Character? 28
    Religion and Politics in England 32

4. Family and Relationships *34*
    Mary's Right to Rule England 34
    Mary and Elizabeth's Relationship 36

5. Mary's Return to Scotland *38*
    Mary's Marriage to Lord Darnley 39

6. The Murder of David Rizzio and Birth of Mary's Son .. *46*

7. Exit Lord Darnley and Enter the Earl of Bothwell *59*

8. The End Game in Scotland *65*
    Imprisonment in Lochleven Castle 65
    The Battle of Langside 68

9. Mary's Last Night in Scotland *71*

10. Mary's Life After Leaving Scotland *73*
    And What Happened to the Earl of Bothwell? 78

11. Mary and Her Legacy *79*
    What Was Mary Really Like? 79
    Mary's Legacy 81

12. Edinburgh - National Museum of Scotland 83
Appendix 1 - Mary's Timeline 85
Appendix 2 - The Main Scottish Sites Associated with Mary 88
   Summary of the Sites.. 89
   Visiting the Sites 91
      Travelling to the Sites 92
Appendix 3 - Further Reading................................... 93

Mary Queen of Scots
By an unknown artist - Blairs Museum - The Museum of Scotland's Catholic Heritage. Public Domain.
https://commons.wikimedia.org/w/index.php?curid=3686266

Preface

Mary Queen of Scots must rival Robert the Bruce as the most famous Scottish monarch. The period in which she lived was one of the most exciting and turbulent in Scotland's history. And as much of Scotland's history is turbulent, that is quite an accolade.

Scotland's queen from a few days after her birth, at five years old she was sent to the sophisticated court of France for her safety, and in preparation for her marriage to the heir to the French throne. She was for a short time the Queen of France, the most powerful and sophisticated country in Europe at that time.

Mary attempted to rule Scotland at one of the most tempestuous times in its history, in the midst of the Protestant reformation. Mary was a Catholic when many, although not all, of the Scottish nobles were Protestant, a recipe for conflict at a time of religious strife and fanaticism. Catholics and Protestants struggled for supremacy, and both churches were bigoted and intolerant, seeing their rivals as heretics rather than fellow Christians. Mary's task of ruling the country was almost impossible.

In some ways Scotland then was like Afghanistan is today; a country with a weak central government, where much of the real power lay with warlords. Again like Afghanistan the county had been racked by war and the intervention of foreign powers. In Scotland's case then England and France, in Afghanistan's now first Russia and then the West.

Scotland was a small and poor nation. Accurate population figures are not available, but it seems likely that in the middle of the 16th century Scotland's population was about 600,000. England and Wales was about 4,000,000 and France, the European superpower, approaching 20,000,000. Scotland was therefore a relative minnow, but an important minnow as it was on the northern border of England, and therefore able to present a major threat to England when Scotland was allied with France.

Surprisingly for such a Scottish icon, Mary was only to spend just over twelve years of her life in Scotland - five years and eight months before being sent to France, and six years nine months of personal rule when she returned. She spent longer in England, almost twenty years, and in France, thirteen years. Mary's Scottish years were momentous though, and are the main focus of this book.

This is Mary's story, focusing on her life in Scotland.

1. Mary's Early Years

Scotland When Mary Was Born

In the early 1500s Northern Europe was in religious ferment, with the Catholic church being challenged in many countries by the new Protestant religion. This affected Scotland as well, and there was increasing tension between those who supported the new religion, and the supporters of the still dominant Roman Catholic church.

In 1542 when Mary was born, King James V of Scotland, Mary's father, was 30. Unfortunately relations between England and Scotland had broken down yet again. Henry VIII of England had usurped the Pope's authority and taken over what was formerly the Catholic church in England. Henry believed James supported the Pope, and therefore that James was a potential enemy. Many historians believe this was probably the case. This made for a fractious relationship between James and Henry, and therefore Scotland and England.

James had also greatly insulted Henry by not attending a planned meeting with him in York, leaving Henry waiting there. James was concerned that Henry might have kidnapped him, a real danger due to Henry's volatile and unstable temperament.

Relations between England and Scotland deteriorated. There were several border incidents. Henry sent an army into Scotland to teach James a lesson, but this was beaten by the Scots at the battle of Haddon Rig, near Kelso, in August 1542, and it withdrew.

In retaliation for Henry's ill-fated raid into Scotland, James decided that Scotland should raid into England, and he assembled an army of at least 15,000 men. While making its way towards Carlisle, the Scottish army was met by an

English force of about 3,000 at Solway Moss. The English force was largely made up of reivers (borders bandits and raiders), under the command of the English Warden, Henry's key official in the area. The Scottish force's command was divided and morale was low. Common soldiers had no confidence in their leaders, who were James's favourites rather than competent generals. There was a major difference in the quality of leadership of the two armies, and this was to prove decisive, in spite of the huge difference in size of the armies.

The battle was a disaster for Scotland. The Scots were outmanoeuvred, hemmed in by the English army and routed. One estimate is that only twelve Scots and seven English were killed in the battle, but 1,200 Scots were taken prisoner, including many Scottish nobles. Several hundred more Scots were drowned in the River Esk trying to escape.

James, who had been at Lochmaben Castle in the Borders while the fighting took place, retired a broken and ill man to his palace at Falkland in Fife.

Mary's Family and Childhood

James V was married twice, first in 1537 to Madeleine of Valois, a French princess. Madeleine was the daughter of the king of France. She was known to be sickly, and died, possibly of tuberculosis, a few months after moving from France to Scotland's colder and wetter climate.

James's second wife was also French. Marie of Guise was from the powerful and aristocratic Guise family. Marie was attractive, charming, intelligent and became politically astute. However she was a convinced Catholic, a disadvantage towards the end of her life when Scotland was becoming Protestant. She was interested in furthering the influence of France, not always easy when the increasingly Protestant Scotland was turning away from Catholic France and aligning itself more closely with Protestant England.

Before marrying James Marie had been married to Louis, Duke of Longueville. But Louis died of smallpox when Marie was only twenty-one. This left Marie a widow with two young sons, one of whom was to die in infancy. The other she had to leave in France when she moved to Scotland. This son died in boyhood.

Marie was a very eligible widow, and at one time it had been suggested she could be the wife of Henry VIII of England. Henry was reported to have said that he was a big man and needed a big wife. Marie was nearly 6 feet tall, as her daughter Mary was to grow to be. Marie had observed to friends that although she was big, she had but a little neck. This was a reference to Henry's second wife, Anne Boleyn's remark, when she was going to the executioner's block, about having but a little neck. Marie was clearly not attracted to the idea of marrying Henry, who had achieved a reputation throughout Europe for disposing of his wives. But she would not have had much choice if the French king and her family felt it was in their best interests.

Marie gave birth to two sons by James V, but both boys died in infancy within days of each other in April 1541. Her grief must have been overwhelming. Unfortunately such infant deaths were not unusual as the child mortality rate in the 16th century was very high.

Her third child by James V, the princess who was to become Mary Queen of Scots, was born at Linlithgow Palace on 7 December 1542. Mary's father was to live for only seven days after the birth of his daughter. He was very ill with a fever and a deep depression following his army's humiliating defeat. As described earlier he had based himself in Falkland Palace, another royal palace about forty miles from Linlithgow. He may well have gone to Falkland Palace deliberately to avoid passing on his fever to his pregnant wife and daughter. James was never to see his daughter.

James would have preferred a legitimate male heir rather than a daughter. Before Mary was born in addition to the two legitimate children who had died in infancy, the thirty year old king had at least nine illegitimate children, including

Linlithgow Palace, where Mary was born. Now a beautiful ruin.

several sons, by a number of mistresses. But as they were illegitimate they could not inherit the crown.

When James was told of Mary's birth he is reported to have said "*It came wi' a lass, it will go wi' a lass.*" The Stuarts had become Scotland's royal dynasty because an ancestor had married Marjorie Bruce, Robert the Bruce's daughter. Robert the Bruce's male heir died, and therefore the crown passed to the Stuarts because of this marriage. James thought it unlikely that a woman could successfully rule Scotland, and therefore he expected Mary's reign to be short, and for Mary to be the last Stuart monarch.

We do not know exactly where in Linlithgow Palace Mary was born. Linlithgow is now a magnificent ruin, and when Mary was born it would have been a truly magnificent palace. When Mary's mother had first seen the palace she had said it was "as fine as any castle in France". It stands in the small town of Linlithgow, on a slight promontory jutting into Linlithgow Loch (lake). Linlithgow is around half-way between the royal castles of Stirling and Edinburgh, and therefore a good stopping off point for royal parties travelling between the two. It was owned by Mary's mother as part of her marriage contract with James, and she often used it as her main residence.

Mary spent the first seven months of her life in the palace, and was christened in the Church of St Michael just outside the palace walls. Even as an infant the marriage tussle started. Male relatives usually controlled the destiny of royal or aristocratic young women. A young woman was expected to marry a man of similar or higher standing. These marriages were for property, power, alliances, and to continue the male dynasty by having children. The wife was usually the junior partner. If love was also involved that was a happy co-incidence, not a prerequisite. As a queen, Mary was a great prize as she had a kingdom to pass on, and also a strong claim to the English crown. It is to her great credit that she was to rise above her expected role.

Mary's mother, Marie of Guise, very effectively protected the young queen. Following the death of her father there was a dispute amongst the Scottish nobility about who was to be regent and to have custody of Mary. Having custody of Mary could allow the aristocrat to control Scotland by ruling in her name. James Hamilton, the Earl of Arran, wanted to have control of the child. After Mary, Arran could claim the strongest claim to the Scottish throne as he was the great-grandson of James II of Scotland, through his grandmother. As it was through the female, rather than the male line, his claim was weaker than Mary's. In addition there was some question over Arran's legitimacy.

Nonetheless, after Mary, Arran had a strong claim to the throne, and might have inherited it if Mary had died. As child mortality was very high at the time, the death of the child queen could have been explained away. Mary's mother would have been well aware of the fate of the "Princes in the Tower" in London 50 years before. The two legitimate heirs to the

English throne were probably murdered by their uncle, acting as regent and ruling England on their behalf, so that he could inherit the throne. So to ensure her daughter's safety Mary's mother fought a cunning political battle, and managed to retain control of the child.

At the same time Henry VIII, the King of the English superpower on Scotland's border, was becoming increasingly aggressive. After Scotland's defeat at the battle of Solway Moss, and with their King dead and the Scottish army broken, Henry VIII could probably have taken Scotland by force if he wanted to. But, perhaps aware that winning Scotland by force was one thing, but holding it indefinitely against guerrilla warfare would be very costly, Henry came up with a "cunning plan". Henry wanted his five year old son Edward, (Henry had fathered a son by then), to marry the infant Mary when they were of age. That would give Henry and his dynasty control of Scotland.

Many in the Protestant faction in Scotland also wanted Mary to be contracted to marry the English prince. Under Henry VIII England had left the Catholic church, and some amongst Scotland's Protestant faction saw Henry as their ally in their battle against Catholicism. However Mary's mother was a committed Catholic, and French. As well as wanting the best for her daughter, she wanted Scotland to stay Catholic for religious reasons. She also wanted Scotland to be an ally of France, and therefore a potential Catholic threat to England's northern border. So Mary's mother was opposed to the marriage to the English prince.

But for the time being the Scottish parliament was able to get its way, and in July 1543, after much politicking and no doubt bribery by Henry, the seven month old Mary was contracted by the Scottish parliament to marry Prince Edward when she was ten, as part of what was known as the Treaty of Greenwich.

At about that time Marie moved her daughter from Linlithgow to the much more defensible Stirling Castle. The child travelled in a litter with an escort of 3,500 troops provided by the nobles who supported Marie. Such was the risk that the infant queen might be kidnapped.

Stirling Castle stands on a volcanic outcrop, towering over the surrounding area, and Marie knew her daughter would be safer there. Mary did not return to Linlithgow until she came back to Scotland to rule as Queen of Scots in 1561, and even then only for short stays.

There were two groups with a motive for kidnapping the infant queen. Scottish nobles who controlled Mary would be able to exercise power in her name. As mentioned earlier the Earl of Arran was a particular suspect here.

A small "window" was created in the battlements of Stirling Castle so that the infant queen could look out on her realm. It can be seen in the Douglas Garden battlements.

The other main risk was from English agents. They might be under instruction from Henry to transfer her to England before the agreed time for the marriage, to ensure the Scots could not renege on the arrangement. Marie was trying to get the Treaty of Greenwich annulled much against Henry's will, and so the risk from agents in the pay of England was real.

It was an opportune time to move to Stirling Castle. The magnificent renaissance palace that James had ordered to be built within the castle for Marie had just been completed. Therefore they could live within Stirling's powerful defences in great comfort and splendour.

The medieval gate to Stirling Castle. But in Mary's period the towers would have been over twice the height, with conical roofs and would probably have been lime-washed. They were lowered to their current height as part of a later refortification programme, as very tall towers were vulnerable to increasingly powerful artillery.

Mary's Coronation

On 9 September 1543 when she was nine months old, Mary was crowned Queen of Scotland in a Catholic coronation ceremony in the Chapel Royal in Stirling Castle. This building stood in the castle's inner close, and was demolished in the 1590s when a new Chapel Royal was built for the coronation of James VI's son Henry.

Mary's coronation ceremony was intended as a statement of Scotland's power and sophistication, choreographed to impress, and to emphasise Mary's position as queen to her nobles and foreign ambassadors.

The ceremony was conducted by Cardinal David Beaton, the head of the Catholic Church in Scotland. At the coronation the Honours of Scotland, the Scottish crown jewels which had recently been refurbished, were used for the first time together. The Earl of Arran, the noble who was the greatest threat to Mary as he was next in line for the throne, carried the crown. The Earl of Lennox carried the sceptre, and the Earl of Argyll the sword. At the key point in the ceremony Cardinal Beaton could only hold the crown over Mary's head as she was too small to wear it. The young queen was only nine months old, and she cried throughout the ceremony. And well she might. She was inheriting the Scottish crown, a poisoned chalice if ever there was one. Mary's father, James V, was the first James monarch to die of natural causes, and even he had died a broken man because of his army's inglorious defeat at Solway Moss.

The ways that James's ancestors, James I to IV, met their ends give a good indication of the difficulty of ruling Scotland.

James I was stabbed to death in a sewer while trying to escape from a group of rebel nobles.

James II died when one of his cannons exploded at the siege of Roxburgh Castle, which was being held by the English.

James III was killed during, or murdered immediately after, a battle against rebel nobles who wanted James' son to rule instead.

James IV was killed by English soldiers when leading his troops at the Battle of Flodden. James IV was the last British monarch to die in battle. After James, British monarchs either allowed their armies to be led by professional soldiers, or if they did attend the battle, stayed well back!

This was the monarchy that Mary was heir to!

The "Rough Wooing"

Mary stayed at Stirling Castle for her safety. The next four years were a very turbulent time. Increasingly the Protestant religion was taking hold in the country. But the Catholic political faction, supported by Mary's staunchly Catholic mother, was still very powerful and did not want its queen to marry a Protestant. Scottish sentiment in general turned against the marriage to a future king of England, which in practice would have led to England controlling Scotland. Therefore when Henry's forces attacked and seized some Scottish merchant ships, the Scottish government took this as justification for annulling the marriage contract and renewing their alliance with France, much to Henry's fury. The Treaty of Greenwich had only lasted for six months.

Henry was now in his fifties, and increasingly ill, grossly overweight and with an ulcerated and very painful leg. He was extremely bad tempered and, some historians believe, psychotic. Henry became more and more incensed by what he considered the double dealing of the Scots in repudiating the marriage contract.

This resulted in what became known as the "rough wooing". To terrorise the Scots and obtain their agreement to the marriage, Henry sent armies into Scotland. In May 1544 a large English army invaded and laid waste to the city of Edinburgh, although the castle managed to hold out. Henry's orders to his army included the following:

> "Put all to fire and sword, burn Edinburgh, so razed and defaced when you have sacked and gotten what ye can of it, as there may remain forever a perpetual memory of the vengeance of God lightened upon (them) for their falsehood and disloyalty...... and as many towns and villages about Edinburgh as you may conveniently."

Mary and her mother were in the relative safety of Stirling Castle while much of south eastern Scotland and Fife was burned and laid waste by English troops.

There followed eight years of conflict and devastation, particularly in the border area and southeast Scotland. Henry's official in charge of the Borders, Wharton, used bribery and threat to turn many of the Scottish border families against one another, creating a civil war along the border. In the end it achieved nothing except destruction.

But the battles didn't always go one way. In February 1545 a small Scottish force, under Archibald Douglas, 6th Earl of Angus, defeated a much larger English force at Ancrum Moor near Jedburgh. Angus, who had sometimes been allied to Henry VIII, was incensed when English troops despoiled his Douglas family tombs in Melrose Abbey. Henry had also granted some Douglas land to the English commander, Sir Ralph Eure, and Angus threatened that he would witness the title deeds with a sharp pen and red ink! So Angus changed allegiance and was put in charge of the Scottish defenders.

At Ancrum Moor a small Scottish force attacked the English encampment, and was easily driven back by the English. But when the pursuing English crested a hill they found the main body of the Scottish army waiting for them in battle order. The Scots victory over the invaders gave Scotland some respite from English incursions.

Henry VIII, prematurely old, sick, and in pain, died in January 1547. Unfortunately that didn't stop the "rough wooing". Henry's nine year old son succeeded to the throne as Edward VI. But in practice the country was run by Edward's uncle, the Earl of Hertford who promoted himself to Duke of Somerset. He continued the tactic of terror and destruction in Scotland.

In another invasion in 1547 English forces achieved a major victory over the Scottish army at Pinkie Cleugh, about seven miles east of Edinburgh. It was a bloodbath for the Scots. The Scottish Army probably numbered about 35,000, double the size of the English army. But the incompetent Earl of Arran was in charge, and ordered the Scots to leave their defensive position and charge the English positions. The Scots suffered badly from artillery fire from English ships which were following the English army as it advanced along the coast. Arran lost his nerve and chose to leave the field when the fighting became intense, causing a major retreat in the Scottish forces. The retreating Scots were then cut down in their thousands by the English cavalry.

There was a risk that the English army might lay siege to Stirling Castle, where the young Mary was staying. The Scots wanted to avoid their young queen being trapped in Stirling. So Mary was spirited out of the castle on a litter in the dark of night, and sent to Inchmahome Priory. Inchmahome was an Augustinian priory on a small island in the Lake of Menteith, near Aberfoyle. It was only seventeen miles from Stirling, but in a lonely, beautiful and hidden setting at the very foot of the Scottish Highlands. Had English troops managed to find Inchmahome, one option would have been to move Mary into the Highlands. Many of the highland clans would have been prepared to conceal and protect their infant queen, irrespective of the dangers to themselves.

After three weeks at Inchmahome, and after the pillaging English army had left the area, if was felt safe to return Mary to Stirling Castle. However, Stirling Castle did not offer safety in the longer term – English troops were now garrisoned in Southern Scotland, and there was always the risk of them taking to the offensive again. Therefore the decision was taken to move Mary to an even safer place. She was moved to Dumbarton Castle near the mouth of the Firth of Clyde (the estuary of the River Clyde) on Scotland's west coast.

Mary spent five months in Dumbarton Castle, from March 1548 until 29 July 1548, while negotiation took place between Scotland and France about Mary's future. As Mary's mother was a French aristocrat from the powerful Guise family, she was well connected to the French royal family, which must have helped greatly in the negotiations. Mary's mother and the Scottish Parliament agreed that Mary would live under the protection of the French King, Henri II, and when she was old enough she would marry his son François, who was destined to become King of France. In practice this was likely to give France control over Scotland, and create a permanent threat to England's northern border in the on and off war between England and France.

Mary arrived in France in August 1548. She was to be brought up in the French court as a young house guest, or rather palace guest, while waiting to come of age and become the wife of François. Mary left from Dumbarton Castle aged five years seven months on the galleys that had brought a French army to support the Scots against the English army, which still held land in the south and east of Scotland. Mary was accompanied by the "four Maries", Mary Seton, Beaton, Fleming and Livingston. These were the daughters of courtiers and aristocrats, and were around Mary's age, and probably named Mary in honour of Marie of Guise. They accompanied Mary as companions and playmates.

Meanwhile the Scots, bolstered by French troops, got the better of the English army. The main English force in Scotland was besieged in the East Lothian town of Haddington and eventually forced to withdraw.

And so it went on. The English troops in Scotland were reinforced, and for several years much of southern Scotland was again controlled by England. It was a ghastly time of guerrilla warfare, retaliation and atrocities. Eventually England decided that controlling Scotland was not worth the cost, and in 1551 the treaty of Norham was agreed at Norham Castle, a major English castle on the border. The treaty of Norham brought hostilities to an end.

2. Mary in France

In August 1548 the young Mary and her entourage arrived in France. Mary's mother, Marie of Guise, remained in Scotland. She played a weak hand well in order to protect the interests of her daughter in the bear-pit of mid 16th century Scottish politics. Mary and her mother remained very close, and corresponded frequently. They met again two years later in 1550 when Mary's mother visited France for a year. They were never to meet again.

Mary adapted quickly to life in the French court, and seems to have captivated most people around her, including her future father-in-law Henri II of France. Unfortunately she didn't have such success with her future mother-in-law, Henri's wife Catherine de Medici. Mary seems to have been a feisty child. When asked by Catherine de Medici why she did not bow to the Queen of France, it is claimed Mary asked her why she did not bow to the Queen of Scotland.

The mother of Mary Fleming, one of the four Maries, was also called Mary. The mother accompanied the group as the young Queen of Scots' governess. As well as being Mary's governess Mary Fleming was the Queen of Scots aunt, as she was an illegitimate daughter of James IV. She caused a scandal when she had an affair with Henri II and became pregnant. As well as a wife Henri already had an official mistress, both of whom were infuriated by this Scottish interloper! So the young Mary Fleming's mother was sent back to Scotland in disgrace.

In January 1558 Mary's uncle, her mother's brother the Duke of Guise, won a major victory for France by capturing Calais, the last English possession in France, for the French crown.

This increased the standing and popularity of the Guise family with the king and French people. As a result Henri II decided to bring forward Mary's marriage to his son and heir François.

François as drawn by François Clouet

Royal marriages at that time were for power and property, not love. France and many nobles in Scotland saw a closer alliance to be in both countries' best interest. So as arranged between the families, Mary married François in April 1558, in a ceremony in the magnificent Notre-Dame Cathedral in Paris. Mary was fifteen, and François fourteen.

Mary had matured in France into an attractive and

accomplished young woman, and so all attention was focused on the beautiful bride at the wedding. At almost six foot she was very tall by 16th century standards, and had striking auburn hair. Mary towered over her decidedly less attractive groom. François had a limp, was short, shy and a stutterer. It is possible he had not reached puberty, and that the marriage was never consummated. But they had grown up together and seemed to have had a genuine affection for each other.

By marrying Mary, François also acquired a claim to the English throne. As described in more detail in chapter 4, in the view of many Catholics, including English Catholics, Mary had been born third in line to the English throne. When Henry VIII's son Edward, and daughter Mary Tudor were alive, this claim was rather theoretical. However Edward died in 1553 without children, and Mary Tudor died childless in 1558. As described later in more detail in chapter 4, Mary and François then became, in the view of Catholics, the rightful queen and king of England.

Encouraged by François' father, and Mary's French relatives, François and Mary added the English coat of arms to those of Scotland and France on their belongings and property. This declared that they considered themselves to be the rightful monarchs of England. As a planned insult to Elizabeth, Mary's Guise relatives invited the English ambassador to a meal with the young couple, which was served on crockery with the French and English coat of arms. Queen Elizabeth soon became aware of this from her ambassador.

This action was to sour Elizabeth's attitude to Mary for the rest of her life. Elizabeth saw Mary as a real threat to her crown. As will be described in chapter 4 Mary was a great grand-daughter of Henry VII of England and so also had a strong claim on the English throne. Therefore she was a possible rallying point for the large Catholic minority in England, who viewed the Protestant Elizabeth as illegitimate, and consequently unable to be queen.

François became king of France in 1559, much earlier than

expected, when his father Henri died in a jousting accident. He had been jousting with Gabriel de Montgomery, the captain of his Scottish Guard. From the early 1400s Scottish soldiers had formed an elite military unit known for its fighting powers and loyalty, and this was the bodyguard of the French monarch. When Montgomery's lance broke in the joust, a splinter penetrated the king's eye and brain.

François was fifteen when he inherited the crown, and Mary, the new Queen Consort of France, was sixteen. Whilst Mary was the Queen Consort of France, her husband François was granted the crown matrimonial of Scotland, meaning that they ruled Scotland jointly, and in the event of Mary's death François would rule Scotland.

By all accounts Mary had felt very close to her father-in-law Henri. He had acted in many ways as her father from her arrival in France. Mary must have been very saddened by his death, even if it resulted in her becoming Queen of France.

1560 was to bring two other major tragedies in Mary's life. Her mother, Marie of Guise, who had been ruling Scotland on Mary's behalf during much of Mary's minority in France, died on 11 June 1560. Even worse was to follow. Mary's marriage was to be short-lived. Her husband François, whose health had never been good, died on 5 December 1560, just two days before Mary's eighteenth birthday. François died in great pain from an ear infection that led to an abscess in his brain.

Many in Scotland were not unhappy by François's death, particularly in the Protestant faction. It had always been a concern that if Mary and François had a son, he would have grown up in France as a Catholic, destined to rule both Scotland and France. A French Catholic king of Scotland would surely have tried to stamp out the Protestant religion, and to make Scotland a Catholic client of France. How one event can change history!

After her husband's death Mary felt her best option was to return to Scotland. Her marriage contract included a 16th century prenup that stripped her of power on the death of her husband. It soon became clear that her mother-in-law, Catherine de Medici, who then ruled as regent on behalf of her other young son Charles, found Mary an inconvenience, and they disliked each other. Mary was also a Guise. Her position as queen dowager gave the Guise family more status at court, which Catherine de Medici felt gave them too much power and might threaten her ability to rule on behalf of her son.

Mary's kingdom of Scotland had been looked after by her mother, and following her mother's death Mary may have been concerned there was no one to defend her interests. Mary was encouraged to return to rule her Scottish kingdom, and decided to do so.

3. Religion and Politics

Before continuing with Mary's biography, it is useful to understand the key influences on her rule. This chapter considers the religious background in Scotland and England at the time. Chapter 4 considers the second crucial factor, Mary's lineage and her relationship to two of the other leading protagonists, Lord Darnley who was to become her second husband, and Queen Elizabeth I of England.

The Religious Divide in Scotland

From the beginning of the 16th century there was increasing unrest in Northern Europe about corruption in the Catholic church. The church was seen by many people as aloof, having lost its way and acting in the interests of the Church hierarchy, rather than God and the people. Religious tensions were a major cause of discord within Scotland and England and in their relationship with each other.

Religion was something the authorities were prepared to murder for, and some believers were prepared to die for. There were fewer religious martyrs in Scotland than in England, but there were some. In 1546 the charismatic Protestant preacher George Wishart was burnt at the stake outside St Andrews Castle on the orders of Cardinal Beaton, the head of the Catholic church in Scotland, who had presided at Mary's coronation. Beaton had watched the grisly spectacle from the castle. In retaliation, a group of Protestants gained entry to St Andrews Castle disguised as builders, and murdered Cardinal Beaton. This was a major challenge to Catholicism in Scotland. They were joined by John Knox, who had trained as a Catholic priest but in time became a Protestant firebrand. Knox was later to become Mary's main religious tormentor.

Beaton's assassins managed to hold St Andrews Castle for a year against the forces of the then Scottish Catholic government. However they were defeated when French troops and artillery reinforced the castle's attackers. Many of the defenders, including Knox, became French galley slaves. Knox was released after seventeen months. It is not clear why. Some historians suggest that it was because Knox became ill. An alternative theory is that England, which was by then Protestant, paid a ransom for the release of leading Scottish Protestants, as they saw them as possible allies in undermining Catholic power in Scotland.

In 1561 Mary was returning to a land in ferment, which had just undergone a religious revolution. Only the year before, Scotland had officially become Protestant after decades of religious strife. But there was still a large Catholic population, and a great deal of religious discord and intolerance on both sides. Much of the aristocracy were Protestant, some to be part of the winning side and to share in the spoils of Catholic church land and property. But others were true believers.

Mary was Catholic, and insisted on practising her religion, which was illegal for her subjects. But she made it clear from the start (and it was a prerequisite of returning to Scotland as Queen), that she would make no attempt to impose her religion on the people. Although she was a practicing Catholic, during her reign she supported tolerance between the religions.

When Mary Tudor had become queen of England only a decade earlier, she had re-imposed Catholicism on England in a particularly brutal way. However this was ultimately short-lived as she had died childless of natural causes and been succeeded by her half-sister, the Protestant Queen Elizabeth. But because of Mary Tudor's attempt to re-impose Catholicism on England, many of the Queen of Scots' Protestant lords and subjects feared that their queen would try to re-impose Catholicism on them. Their concerns were increased as Mary made the mistake of having too many foreign Catholic courtiers in her entourage, breeding suspicion.

A further difficulty in imposing her rule was Mary's gender. Female rulers had been almost unknown until then. This changed in the middle of the 16th century when England had two queens in succession, Mary Tudor followed by Elizabeth I. And before Mary returned to Scotland, the country had been ruled on her behalf by her mother. But female rule was still new, and the nobles in Scotland are unlikely to have come to terms with this major change. The young Queen of Scots' gender and religion were to prove a strain between her and many of her nobles and subjects.

The other major player in Scottish politics was France. France was predominantly Catholic, with a Protestant minority, called Huguenots. By some assessments Huguenots made up to fifteen percent of the population of France at their peak. France was a hotbed of religious intolerance, the most significant event of which was known as the St Bartholomew's Day massacre.

On St Bartholomew's Day 1572 many thousands of Huguenot men, women and children, some of them attending a royal wedding in Paris, were murdered as part of a preplanned crime motivated by religious intolerance. By then Mary was a captive in England, but the massacre strengthened feelings against her as she was a Catholic and her Guise relations in France had been involved in planning the massacre.

It is very easy to criticise the apparent religious intolerance of people in the 16th century, and much of the criticism is justified. However the stakes for the key players could be extremely high. If the adherents of one religion were to gain power, the result might have been a horrible death for some Christians on the other side of the religious divide (or chasm). The fear of that happening could result in polarised and adversarial positions being taken, even by otherwise reasonable people, not just by fanatics.

John Knox - a (K)noxious Character?

John Knox was a very important figure in the Scottish reformation, and therefore in Scottish church history. He was

Mary's main Protestant tormentor, convinced that women should not be in a position of power, and that Mary's agenda was to return Scotland to Catholicism. Because he was so significant to Mary's story, it is worthwhile learning a little about him.

Knox had trained as a Catholic priest, although because of a lack of openings in the church he began his career by practising as the 16th century equivalent of a country lawyer instead. In time he became convinced that the Protestant religion was far closer to the bible than Catholicism.

Many people see Knox as a religious fanatic. He was dogmatic and inflexible, and became fervently anti-Catholic. He played a major part in overthrowing Catholicism in Scotland, and ensuring Scotland became a Presbyterian, rather than an Anglican Protestant country.

So what were the differences between the two Protestant churches? The Anglican church still has a hierarchy of bishops, like the Catholic church. The monarch is head of the Anglican church, although that is rather theoretical today. Some Anglican rites are similar to Catholic rites. The Presbyterian style of Protestant worship that Knox championed and helped implement emphasises the authority of the bible, and that the church be run by its congregation and elders, rather than bishops. It does not acknowledge the authority of the monarch in religious matters.

But Knox was to change Scottish history in a much wider sphere than religion. Knox and his co-religionists were very much in favour of education. They believed that every child should be taught to read. This would allow them to read the bible, rather than have it interpreted for them by a priesthood, as happened in the Catholic Church of the time. Knox wanted every parish to have a school, and while this was not achieved for many decades, he made a start.

Because of Knox and other Protestants placing such importance on education, by the 18th century Scotland was the most literate nation in the world. Such a literate society needed universities, and for many years Scotland had five (Edinburgh, Glasgow, St Andrews and two in Aberdeen), whereas the much more highly populated England only had two (Oxford and Cambridge). Also many of the Scottish universities were considered to be world class, while for some time the English universities were not.

During what is known as the Scottish Enlightenment in the 18th century, the country was a global leader and made a major contribution to science, medicine, philosophy and thinking. In fact Scots largely invented the sciences of economics (Adam Smith), and geology (James Hutton). Because they were highly literate Scots could be excellent administrators, and played a major part in administering the British empire. All this was based on a foundation of widespread education, a consequence of Knox and his co-religionists' focus on education so that ordinary people could read the bible.

But Knox lacked what today would be described as emotional intelligence. Had he tried to persuade Mary, rather than harangue her, it may have been possible to bridge some of the religious differences between Mary and the Protestants. Knox also taught that the people had the right to overthrow their rulers if their rulers were corrupt or immoral. (By his definition of corruption or immorality of course.) This was a revolutionary doctrine for the time, and was to cause a conflict with Mary, who although tolerant and kindly, had a firm view of her rights as queen. For the same reasons Knox offended Elizabeth I.

His detractors argue that Knox was a misogynist and hypocrite. He wrote a scathing attack on female rulers. In his fifties he married a young woman of seventeen, which led some critics viewing his puritanical moralising as hypocrisy.

Knox was a complex character, a mixture of good and bad. But his emphasis on widespread literacy was to change the history of Scotland, and result in the huge impact this small country was to have on the world.

John Knox's statue in Edinburgh University's New College quadrangle, in Mound Place, Edinburgh. Knox was a charismatic preacher, but dogmatic and intolerant.

Religion and Politics in England

Henry VIII's reign had been a time of great religious change in England. Henry had been desperate to have a son. He had a daughter by his first wife, Catherine of Aragon, but in the early 1500s female rulers were rare, and Henry could only be confident about his dynastic succession if he had a son. After many years Henry decided the only solution to his dynastic problem was to marry a younger wife capable of providing him with more children. Because he could not get the Pope to agree to him divorcing Catherine, Henry eventually took control of the Catholic Church in England and changed it to a quasi-Protestant church. He then divorced Catherine. But the divorce was not recognised by most Catholics, and therefore they considered any children Henry had while Catherine was alive to be illegitimate. Illegitimate children were not entitled to inherit the crown.

Henry's actions in taking over the Catholic Church in England also allowed him to expropriate the church's vast assets and income. It has been estimated that between a quarter and a fifth of land in England was owned by the church. So becoming quasi-Protestant greatly helped Henry's exchequer.

When Henry died he was succeeded by his son Edward, who was only nine at the time. Edward's legitimacy was not in doubt, as Henry had no living ex-wives when he married his third wife, Jane Seymour, Edward's mother. (Henry's first wife Catherine of Aragon had died by then, and he had his second wife Anne Boleyn beheaded.) Edward was strongly influenced by his advisors, who were committed Protestants. But Edward was stricken with tuberculosis, and only ruled from 1547 to 1553. After Edward's death there was an attempt by the English Protestant nobility to put the young and innocent Lady Jane Grey, Henry VIII's great-niece rather than direct descendant, on the throne. Her brief reign of nine days resulted in a Catholic revolt, and in the tragic and innocent Lady Jane ultimately being beheaded.

The revolt resulted in Mary Tudor, the child by Henry's first marriage to Catherine of Aragon, becoming queen. Mary Tudor was fanatically Catholic, and tried to turn the country back to Catholicism. She married Prince Philip of Spain, which caused considerable anger amongst many Protestants in England, and a revolt which she managed to put down. Her marriage took place in Winchester, because of concern that it would not be possible to control the riots that were likely to arise in the much more highly populated London if the marriage took place there.

Mary's methods of trying to impose Catholicism were often bloody, and many leading and some ordinary Protestants were burnt at the stake. She is now known as Bloody Mary.

Mary Tudor was nearly forty when she married, as when they were alive her father and brother had not permitted her to marry. She had a number of false pregnancies but did not have any children. When she died in 1558 she was succeeded by her half-sister Elizabeth, the daughter from Henry's marriage to Anne Boleyn. Elizabeth was Protestant, but not as fanatically Protestant as her sister Mary was fanatically Catholic. But this change of state religion still resulted in the deaths of several hundred Catholics, particularly when the Pope excommunicated Elizabeth. By excommunicating Elizabeth it became legitimate for Catholics, in their eyes, to try to overthrow her. So the excommunication resulted in a number of plots that were put down, and to a sometimes bloody crackdown on Catholicism.

Elizabeth had been Queen of England for three years when Mary Stuart returned to Scotland to rule as queen.

Complex, isn't it? It could also be deadly significant for the aristocracy and population because they were at risk if their religion was not the official religion of the time. As I noted earlier, being the "wrong" religion could result in you losing land and possessions, being forced into exile, or even in extreme cases being beheaded or burnt at the stake.

4. Family and Relationships

Mary's Right to Rule England

The second key to understanding the forces that influenced Mary's reign is to understand her place in the English and Scottish royal families. We shall therefore divert from Mary's life story to consider her right to the crown of England.

This is complicated, so I have included a schematic on the next page. Mary, Lord Darnley, and Elizabeth I are all descendants of Henry VII of England, the more famous Henry VIII's father. This played an important part in the political power struggle which was shortly to engulf Mary.

Mary Queen of Scots was Henry VII of England's great granddaughter. Henry VII's daughter Margaret Tudor, who was Henry VIII's older sister, had married James IV of Scotland. Their son was James V, Mary's father.

Lord Darnley, Mary's second husband will shortly play a major part in this story. He was also a great grandchild of Henry VII. After James IV of Scotland died at the battle of Flodden, James' widow, Margaret Tudor as she had been before her marriage to James IV, married Archibald Douglas, the 6th Earl of Angus. Their daughter, Margaret Douglas, was Darnley's mother. Therefore Darnley was Henry VII's great-grandson, and he had a strong claim to the English throne through his grandmother Margaret Tudor.

A third main character was **Elizabeth I** of England. Elizabeth was Henry VII's granddaughter. Her father was Henry VIII, and her mother Henry's second wife Anne Boleyn.

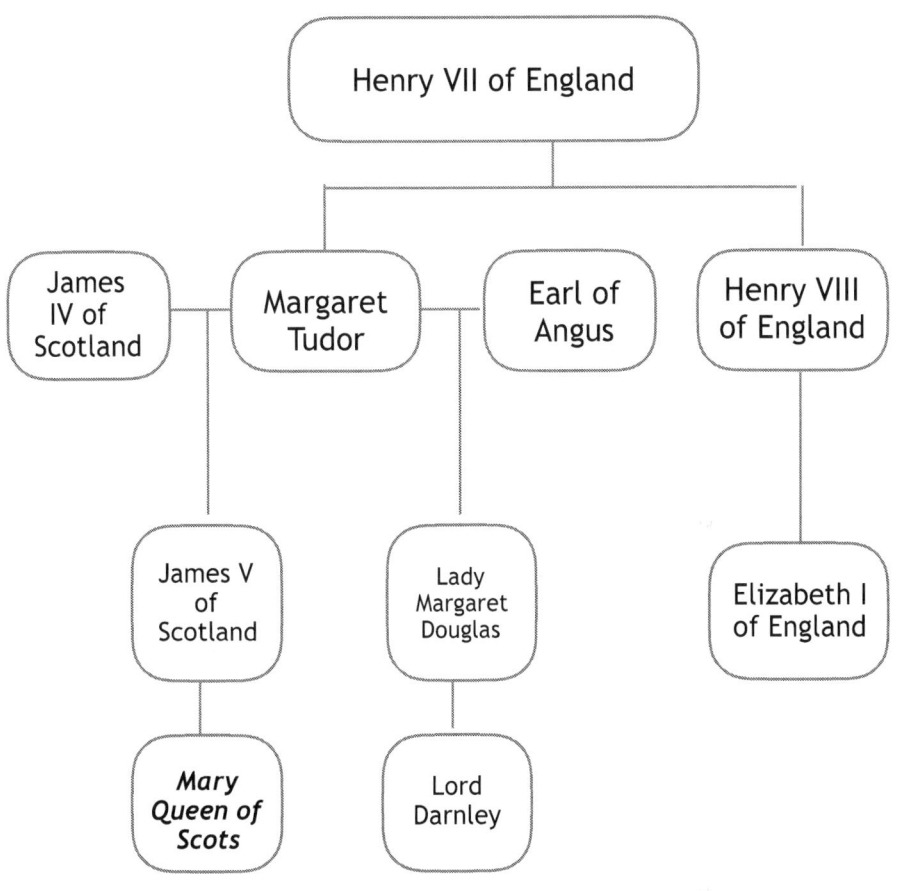

The above abbreviated schematic illustrates the relationship between Mary, Lord Darnley and Elizabeth I. In summary: Margaret Tudor, Henry VIII's sister, and Elizabeth I's aunt, married twice. First to King James IV of Scotland, and after he was killed at the battle of Flodden to Archibald Douglas, Earl of Angus. Margaret Tudor was Mary and Darnley's grandmother, although their grandfathers were different.

As mentioned in the previous chapter Elizabeth's right to inherit the English throne was questioned by many people, especially Catholics. Henry VIII had broken from the Catholic church and divorced his first wife Catherine of Aragon, before marrying Anne Boleyn. Elizabeth was the child of Henry's union with Anne.

Catholics did not recognise Henry's divorce from Catherine of Aragon, and therefore in their view Elizabeth I of England was illegitimate. Many Catholics referred to her as the daughter of "the king's whore". Illegitimate children could not inherit the crown, unless they had a large army on their side!

Mary and Elizabeth's Relationship

Mary Queen of Scots, because of her legitimate descent from Henry VII, was in the opinion of many Catholics the rightful Queen of England, rather than Elizabeth. So, as well as being a relative, Mary was a potential threat to Elizabeth. Unfortunately Mary did nothing to allay Elizabeth's concerns. If Mary had only renounced any claim to the English throne while Elizabeth was alive, this might have greatly influenced the way Elizabeth treated her and dealt with her.

Although Mary and Elizabeth never actually met, they communicated frequently. Elizabeth could be friendly on the surface, but often she tried to be controlling and to undermine Mary.

Unlike Mary, Elizabeth also had very competent advisors to support her, particularly William Cecil, Lord Burghley. Cecil was politically astute, a convinced Protestant who would stop at nothing to support Elizabeth against Catholic plotting, both real and imagined. He did what he could to turn Elizabeth against Mary, as he saw Mary as a real threat.

But there seems to have been some real affection between the two women, after all they were both related and shared the challenge of being female rulers in a man's world.

There was also a great and almost childish rivalry between

them. For example, Elizabeth asked James Melville, the Scottish ambassador to England, who was the fairest queen. Melville answered diplomatically that his queen was the fairest in Scotland and Elizabeth the fairest in England. Elizabeth then asked Melville who was the tallest. Melville answered that Mary was. Elizabeth answered that then Mary was overly high, whilst she was neither over high or over low!

In fact Elizabeth was marked by smallpox scars and wore layers of make-up. Elizabeth had nearly died from smallpox in October 1562. Mary was tall, slim, with beautiful auburn hair, and well developed charm and deportment, clearly the more attractive of the two queens.

Mary returned to rule Scotland aged on eighteen. Elizabeth was nine years her senior. This, together with Elizabeth's considerable political acumen as a result of being brought up amongst the political infighting of Henry VIII's court, and her more competent advisors, gave her an advantage over Mary. But the age difference also meant that it was likely that Elizabeth would die before Mary. If Elizabeth died without an heir, Mary's claim on the English throne was very strong.

5. Mary's Return to Scotland

Mary returned to Scotland on 19 August 1561, after thirteen years in France. Mary was eighteen years old, and in many ways a young French aristocrat. Mary was also a fairly rich young widow, as the marriage contract to her husband had allowed her to keep an income from some properties in France in the event of his death.

The two galleys carrying the royal party landed at Leith, Edinburgh's port. It was a grey, misty morning, which some people took as a bad omen. The galleys had made good time, and arrived several days earlier than expected, so there was no welcoming party to greet Mary. However, when the city became aware of her arrival a large crowd formed and cheered their beautiful young queen. In the circumstances, it was a good start.

Soon Mary and her court took up residence in the Palace of Holyroodhouse. In Mary's time the Palace of Holyroodhouse was a little outside the city walls, which ended down the Royal Mile at the Netherbow Port (gate), near where the World's End pub now stands. This was to be Mary's home in Edinburgh, except when she felt in need of the security provided by the more austere and windswept but highly defensible castle.

In some ways the Scottish nobility (really warlords), tried to accommodate Mary. They had agreed that she could practise her Catholic religion provided she did so in private, a privilege not given to any other person in Scotland.

Trouble arose when Mary took mass in her quarters on her first Sunday back in Scotland. A crowd gathered and threatened the priest and a servant carrying the altar pieces. Mary's illegitimate half-brother Lord James Stuart stood guard outside to ensure she wasn't interrupted. When challenged by the crowd, Lord James craftily justified his presence by saying he was standing guard to ensure no Scotsman could hear the mass!

In her first years back in Scotland Mary travelled widely as part of royal tours, or progresses as they were called. These were intended to show Mary to her nobles, and to help her to forge relationships with them. She travelled extensively in the lowlands, including Fife, in the Borders, and up the east coast as far north as Dingwall. However, Mary did not visit the real Highlands, the Hebrides, or the Orkneys and Shetlands. Mary was an accomplished horsewoman, and usually travelled on horseback, as Scotland's roads were of such a poor quality as to make travel by carriage problematic.

But in many respects Mary was an innocent. She had been trained in France to be queen consort, that is to be the wife of the king, but not to rule herself. She was well versed in languages, deportment, courtly manners, embroidery, dancing and music. But in Scotland she was queen regnant, that is she was the ruler. Mary had not been trained in the skills necessary to rule a country like Scotland, where most of the power lay with warlords, who changed alliances frequently to increase their power or wealth.

Mary's Marriage to Lord Darnley

A fundamental job of any king or queen was to get married and have a son to continue the dynasty. So Mary and her advisers searched for a suitable marriage partner for the young and attractive widowed Queen of Scots. Don Carlos of Spain seemed a possibility, as heir to the dominant Catholic power in Europe. However as he was a Catholic this would have been very unpopular with the Scottish nobles, and in any event, negotiations ended when it became clear he was insane.

Queen Elizabeth of England tried to fob Mary off with Robert Dudley, Earl of Leicester, one of her old paramours, much to

Mary's annoyance. Bizarrely, Elizabeth suggested that Mary move to London, and the three of them live together with Elizabeth footing the bills. A very strange proposal, which Mary rejected.

In February 1565 Mary was greatly taken with the young Henry Stuart, Lord Darnley. Darnley, although of a prominent Scottish family, the Lennox Stuarts, had been born in Yorkshire when his parents had been forced to leave Scotland because they had supported the English side in the Rough Wooing conflict. Darnley had lived in France and England. With the connivance of his parents he made his way to Scotland in the hope of attracting the queen.

> ### Stewart or Stuart?
> Mary's father and his ancestors spelled their name Stewart, but Mary decided to change the spelling to Stuart when she was in France. The letter w is rare in French, and is often pronounced as v, so by changing to Stuart Mary avoided any confusion. Mary's second husband, Henry Stewart/Stuart, more commonly known as Lord Darnley, changed the spelling of his surname to Stuart as well. And therefore we have a Stuart, rather than a Stewart, dynasty.
>
> For simplicity I have used Stuart throughout this text, even for early monarchs.

As noted earlier Mary was related to Darnley, and he also had a claim to the English throne. But only Mary was descended from Margaret Tudor's marriage to James IV. And Mary's claim to the English throne was stronger than Darnley's as her descent from Margaret Tudor was via the male line, rather than the female line. But any child they had together would have an even stronger claim to the English throne than they had individually.

Superficially Darnley was an attractive young man, good

Lord Darnley
By unknown author [Public domain], via Wikimedia Commons

looking if rather effeminate. Sir James Melville, one of Mary's advisors, described Darnley as beardless and lady faced, and there were rumours he was bisexual. But he was well trained in courtly manners and skills such as dancing from his time at the English and French courts. Darnley was also tall. Mary described him to a friend as "the properest and best-proportioned long man that ever she had seen". Mary was almost six feet tall, so would no doubt have appreciated having a tall man as partner!

Darnley had been brought up as a Catholic, but didn't seem to have any difficulty with the Anglicism of Elizabeth I when he was in her court. Religion didn't seem to play a big part in his life. However he was notionally Catholic.

After something of a whirlwind romance Mary married Darnley in a Catholic ceremony on 29 July 1565 at the Palace of Holyroodhouse. The marriage was certainly rushed. Because Mary and Darnley were related, as a Catholic Mary should have obtained a dispensation from the Pope. Mary was not prepared to wait. Luckily the dispensation arrived, but not until the couple were married.

Darnley was nineteen when they married, Mary was twenty-three. It is possible that Mary was still a virgin. Her first husband François had been sickly. He was a year younger than Mary and pictures show François looking younger than his years. He may not have entered puberty before he died, aged only sixteen.

The superficially handsome and attractive Darnley was in fact spoilt, bullying, immature, a heavy drinker, sexually promiscuous and easily manipulated by people ill-disposed to Mary. Had the courtship been longer, Mary might have recognised Darnley's many and manifest faults before the marriage rather than afterwards. But she was a healthy young woman of twenty-three and Darnley was at first sight an attractive young man. Passion prevailed and she didn't wait. As the saying goes, "Marry in haste, repent at leisure".

Another issue was that Darnley was from the powerful

Lennox Stuart family, which had many enemies amongst the Scottish nobility, including the powerful Hamilton family, whose leader was the Earl of Arran. This wouldn't help ensure a smooth reign.

Mary's illegitimate half-brother James Stuart, the Earl of Moray, was against the marriage. Shortly after the marriage he tried to organise a coup against Mary and Darnley. Moray was later to claim that he did this because he was concerned that they would reintroduce Catholicism. The Earl of Moray was a Protestant by conviction, not just convenience.

Before the marriage Moray had been Mary's principle advisor, and it is likely he was also concerned that after the marriage he would be marginalised as Darnley became increasingly influential. In addition Darnley's arrogance and self-centred approach had not helped their relationship. Darnley had loudly declared that he believed Mary had given Moray too many titles and too much land. The silly boy had made a powerful enemy.

Moray, with help from the Earl of Arran, whose Hamilton family was a long-time enemy of Darnley's family, assembled a force in Ayr on the west coast of Scotland. Mary mustered her own force, and was able to assemble an army five times the size of Moray's. Wearing a steel helmet and with a pistol in her belt, Mary displayed a very active and energetic part of her character. She led her army in a fruitless attempt to stage a decisive battle with Moray's force. However, Moray's force managed to slip past Mary's and enter Edinburgh. Although they entered the town, the castle refused to submit to them, and the townspeople made it clear they supported Mary. The coup attempt degenerated into farce, and became known as the Chase-about Raid.

Moray initially withdrew to Dumfries, but in the end had no option but to escape to England. Mary banished him from Scotland, until it became politically necessary for her to allow him to return because of pressures from Moray's supporters in the aristocracy.

Mary and Darnley's marriage quickly soured. A great point of conflict between them was that Darnley wanted the crown matrimonial, and initially Mary promised him this. The crown matrimonial meant that rather than just being the queen's consort, Darnley would be joint ruler whilst she was alive and rule as king in the event of her death. However, it soon became clear to Mary that he was not fit for this honour and responsibility. It would have been dangerous to give more power to this immature and unstable young man.

However, Darnley probably fulfilled one important function. Within a few months of the marriage Mary was pregnant. See the next chapter for an explanation of why I have used the word "probably".

James Stuart, Earl of Moray

James Stuart was one of Mary's illegitimate half-brothers, both Mary and Moray having James V as father. James V had at least nine illegitimate children when he died aged thirty – he was productive in that area! He arranged for two of them to become abbots of Melrose and Kelso abbeys, and for James to become Prior of St Andrews' Cathedral's Priory when aged six. This provided James with an income, but also showed how corrupt the Catholic church had become. James was the most competent and intelligent of James V illegitimate children. He became a convinced Protestant, and supported the Reformation.

James Stuart was to become something of a pain in Mary's neck. He had been instrumental in her return to Scotland, and had negotiated with the Scottish Protestant Lords so that she could continue to celebrate Catholic mass in her private chapel at the Palace of Holyroodhouse. He had been very helpful to Mary at first, and she made him Earl of Moray a year after she returned to Scotland. But Moray and her second husband Lord Darnley became sworn enemies, and Moray changed to opposing her.

Mary was to be avenged for Moray's scheming, although she had no part in planning or carrying out the deed. In 1570 Moray was acting as Regent, ruling Scotland on behalf of Mary's son, the young James VI. Moray became the first head of state to be assassinated by a firearm, when one of Mary's supporters shot him as he was travelling in procession through Linlithgow.

6. The Murder of David Rizzio and Birth of Mary's Son

Only a little over seven months after Mary and Darnley's marriage, the Palace of Holyroodhouse was the site of one of the most dramatic incidents in what was a very dramatic reign. By 1566 the Protestant Lords, and Mary's husband Lord Darnley, had become increasingly envious of the influence of Mary's Italian secretary, David Rizzio.

Rizzio was comparatively lowly born, and had come to Scotland as part of the entourage of a visiting Italian count. Rizzio was short and probably not particularly good looking, but he had a good bass voice which Mary needed for her choir. He was well educated, speaking several languages fluently, a useful skill for the personal secretary he was to become.

Mary must have felt very alone and vulnerable at the time. Her husband was an immature drunkard and her parents were dead. She had no one she could really trust and confide in who was experienced enough to advise her. In a short time Rizzio had ingratiated himself with her, rising from the choir to be her personal secretary, dealing with her sensitive correspondence and controlling access to her.

Whilst able to charm Mary, Rizzio dealt insensitively with the Scottish aristocracy. He was patronising and condescending towards them, and used his position of influence with Mary to take bribes to allow access to her. Scottish Protestant nobles were also concerned that Rizzio might be an agent of the Pope, intent on restoring Catholicism. They therefore wanted to get rid of what they considered to be a lowly born foreign Catholic upstart with too much influence over the queen.

Lord Darnley was also jealous of Rizzio. By this time Mary was pregnant with the future James VI of Scotland and I of England, and there were rumours that Rizzio, and not Darnley, was the father of Mary's unborn child. Whilst this was possible it seems very unlikely. There were also rumours that Darnley had had a homosexual affair with Rizzio. Many events in Mary's reign make modern soap operas look so tame!

Some key Scottish Lords decided to act. They managed to inflame the jealousy of the easily led Lord Darnley and involve him in their plot. Mary documented her version of events in a number of letters, and before he died of cancer Lord Ruthven, one of the chief plotters, recorded his version. Mary's secretary during the later years of her life, Claude Nau, also recorded Mary's version of events in his biography of her, so we have several sources to draw on.

On 9 March 1566 Mary and several friends, including Rizzio, were dining in a small side room off Mary's bedroom in her apartments at Holyroodhouse, when they were joined by Darnley. Darnley had come up a private flight of stairs from his apartment, which was on the floor immediately below Mary's. Mary was surprised to see Darnley, and horrified when he was followed by the macabre figure of Lord Ruthven. Ruthven was wearing a steel helmet, and full armour under his cloak. He was rumoured to be a warlock, and as he was suffering from cancer he had a gaunt and yellow complexion. Ruthven was quickly joined by more conspirators. They

The tower at Holyroodhouse, which contained Mary and Darnley's apartments, and where Rizzio was murdered.

started to drag the hapless Rizzio from the room. Rizzio, realising what was intended, cried out to Mary for help and grabbed onto her skirts.

In the commotion the dining table was overturned. In the eerie half-light given off by the fire, Rizzio, screaming "Justice! Justice! Save me my lady! I am a dying man!" was dragged through the Queen's bedroom to the Queen's outer chamber. He was stabbed to death there, with over 50 knife wounds – it was a bloody affair. Mary didn't see him being murdered, but have heard his screams.

Holyroodhouse
A visit to Holyroodhouse is a must for a Mary enthusiast. Darnley's apartment, the private staircase, Mary's bedroom, the small supper room, and the room where Rizzio was stabbed to death, can be visited as part of the standard Palace of Holyroodhouse tour. These rooms are furnished insofar as possible as they were in Mary's time. They also have a display of memorabilia of Mary and the era.
A tip for the visitor. Mary's apartments are the highlight of the palace and always busy with tourists. After several visits when I felt I couldn't really enjoy them because of the crowds, I found the best approach was to get to the palace when it opened, and to go quickly through the visitors' route directly to Mary's apartments. This allowed me to arrive there before other visitors, who had stopped to examine other parts of the Palace. After enjoying the surroundings and atmosphere of Mary's apartments in peace and tranquillity, you can then move on to the remains of Holyrood abbey, again staying ahead of the multitude of tourists. It is of course possible then to retrace your steps and view the other, more recent, parts of the palace.

There may have been a further agenda for the murder. It is possible that Darnley and the Lords wanted Mary, then six months pregnant, to miscarry, or for her and the baby to be murdered. Mary also claimed that a pistol was put against her pregnant stomach, and the trigger pulled but it failed to fire. Ruthven was to deny this. Mary certainly thought that the conspirators intended to kill her and the baby. Darnley may have felt that the baby could have been Rizzio's rather than his. His other fear may have been that following the birth the baby would be first in line for the throne should Mary die.

The Earls of Bothwell, Huntley and Atholl were also staying in the palace. They weren't involved in the plot, and when they heard the commotion managed to escape to their castles. This put Mary's potential supporters out of the reach of the conspirators.

It seems the conspirators had a clear idea of what to do after the murder. Ruthven claimed that they intended to hold Mary under house arrest in Stirling Castle, where she would look after her baby, while Darnley, as king, would rule with the nobles. Since Darnley was weak and malleable, in practice power would have rested with the nobles.

Darnley was beginning to realise that the conspirators did not trust him, and that they saw him as a pawn, rather than as their king. He was afraid of a group of men who saw murder as an acceptable tool to rid themselves of someone they considered an inconvenience. This young man (he was a very immature 20) felt very vulnerable.

Mary started to think with the political acumen that a 16th century monarch of Scotland needed. Using her guile Mary persuaded Darnley it was in his best interests to change sides and throw in his lot with her. To persuade him they still had a future as King and Queen together she agreed to resume their marital relationship. However luckily for Mary his propensity to get drunk resulted in him falling into a drunken slumber in his room rather than joining her that night.

Next Mary had to avoid being sent to Stirling Castle, where she would find escape very difficult. In Holyroodhouse she had many servants and friends who would help her if they could, and Holyroodhouse was essentially a palace, not a fortress. So Mary pretended that she might be going into labour. The conspirators then allowed her servants access to her, and gave her the privacy to plot.

Later that day she met her half-brother the Earl of Moray, her adversary in the Chase-about raid, whom she had banished. The conspirators had been in touch with him, and had secretly invited him to return to Scotland. She also led the conspirators to believe that she would pardon them, an insincere act, intended to reassure them while she plotted her next move.

She was really getting the hang of being a 16th century Scottish monarch.

Mary's next move was to escape in the middle of the night with Darnley and some supporters, by the same stairway that Rizzio's assassins had used to enter Mary's suite of rooms. They went through Darnley's apartments and the servant quarters, helped by Mary's loyal servants. Outside the palace more of Mary's supporters were waiting with horses. In the dead of night they left Edinburgh, and within a few miles met the Earl of Bothwell, one of her strongest supporters, and an escort to take her to safety.

It must have been an exhausting ride for the six month pregnant young woman. Darnley, ever the coward rode ahead, trying to get himself as far away from danger as possible. When he had to stop to let the party protecting Mary catch up, he told Mary to ride more quickly, and said that if the baby died they could have more! Such was the man.

Eventually they arrived at Dunbar, a strong castle on the coast 25 miles south east of Edinburgh, and controlled by Bothwell. In the following days the number of Mary's supporters swelled as more and more nobles, in this world of shifting alliances, decided to back the queen. Soon they felt strong enough to march on Edinburgh.

The tables were turned, and the key conspirators, Ruthven and Morton, found their support ebbing away and Edinburgh turning against them. They had no alternative but to escape to England. Ruthven died a few months later of the cancer that was consuming his body. James Douglas, the Earl of Morton, was still to play a significant part in Scotland's history, including being regent during part of the minority of Mary's son, but that is another story.

Mary did not miscarry as a result of the shocking events that had occurred. On 15 June 1566, three months after Rizzio's murder, after a difficult labour Mary gave birth to the future James VI of Scotland and I of England, in a small room in the comparative safety of the Palace within Edinburgh Castle. The

James Hepburn, the Earl of Bothwell
By Unknown (Scottish) - iQFMpXROf6j7Ig at Google Cultural Institute, Public Domain,
https://commons.wikimedia.org/w/index.php?curid=21865933

room still exists and is open to visitors. She was safe for the time being, and had achieved a key objective of any female royal at the time - she had successfully produced a male heir.

Mary was disillusioned with Darnley, and had become increasingly romantically attracted to James Hepburn, the Earl of Bothwell. Bothwell was one of Scotland's most powerful Earls, and was Captain of Hermitage Castle, set in a small valley just off Liddesdale in the borders. Liddesdale was the most lawless valley in the Scottish borders, which really says something, as law and order was a rare commodity in the borders at that time. Hermitage provided protection for anyone trying to police this dangerous place.

The Earl of Bothwell's control of Hermitage resulted in one of Hermitage's most famous incidents. In October 1566, just seven months after Rizzio's murder, Bothwell was injured in a skirmish with Little Jock Elliot of Park, a reiver (the common term for a bandit or raider along the Anglo-Scottish border). The wounded Bothwell was taken to his castle of Hermitage. Mary, who had been linked romantically with Bothwell, was in Jedburgh about 25 miles away, on a royal tour of the Borders. When Mary heard of Bothwell's injury, she made the 25 mile journey with a small party to Hermitage to see him. After two hours with Bothwell, Mary rode back the 25 miles to Jedburgh. She may have had pressing business in Jedburgh, or considered it inappropriate to spend the night in the castle.

Hermitage Castle, a grim, bleak castle near the border, designed for war rather than comfort.

These would have been very difficult and exposed journeys across bleak moorland in October. On the return journey her horse threw her in a boggy area now known as the Queen's Mire. In 1817 a watch was found by a shepherd in earth dug up by a mole. This was identified by experts as having been made in France in the 16th century, and is thought to have belonged to Mary. It is on display in Mary Queen of Scots House in Jedburgh, a house where Mary may have stayed, and which is now a museum dedicated to her life.

Any visitors to Jedburgh should also see Jedburgh Abbey, only a few hundred yards from Mary Queen of Scots' House and another victim of Mary's era. The Abbey was damaged by Henry VIII's forces in 1544, and again in 1545, as part of the "rough wooing" which was described in chapter 1. This was when Mary was an infant, and Henry VIII ordered his troops to terrorise Scotland, to try to force the Scots to allow their infant queen to marry his son Edward when they were of age.

When back in Jedburgh, Mary took ill with a fever that nearly killed her. Much later, whilst the long-term prisoner of her cousin Elizabeth, Mary said that she wished she had died at Jedburgh.

After her illness and a tour of the Borders, Mary decided to go to Craigmillar Castle to recuperate. Craigmillar Castle is now within Edinburgh, but in Mary's time Edinburgh was very much smaller and the castle stood about four miles outside the city. Mary was a guest there often, and was a close friend of its laird, Sir Simon Preston. Sir Simon had accompanied her to France, attending her wedding to François, and returned with her to Scotland after François' death. Mary clearly enjoyed visiting Craigmillar, outside the crowded and smelly city, and away from many of her troubles.

When Mary visited Craigmillar she was an exhausted and sick woman. Her short marriage had irrevocably broken down. In March 1566 her secretary had been dragged from her presence and brutally murdered, and her own life had been in danger.

In June she had given birth to her only child, the future James VI of Scotland and I of England. In October Mary had been very ill and almost died. She was exhausted and probably suffering from post-natal depression. She decided to stay at Craigmillar for three weeks to take stock and recuperate.

Mary Queen of Scots' House, Queen Street, Jedburgh. Mary may have stayed here during her visit to Jedburgh. It is now an excellent museum and visitors' centre dedicated to Mary and her life.

The remains of Jedburgh Abbey Church, which was only part of the massive abbey complex. Most of the buildings were burnt down by Henry VIII's troops in 1544, and then again in 1545. Still impressive, it must have been magnificent in its heyday.

Craigmillar Castle in Edinburgh as it is today. Well worth a visit.

By December, although Mary was still ill, she was to enjoy a great triumph, her son the future James VI's christening. This was a major demonstration of "soft power" and status, and also of her superiority to Elizabeth, who of course was unmarried and childless. In spite of the "virgin queen" spin her advisors tried to promulgate, this would at that time have been seen as a major failure for a monarch. In fact, when Elizabeth was told of the birth she is reported to have said that "the Queen of Scots was mother of a fair son, while she was of barren stock."

The christening in Stirling on 17 December 1566 was a major event, attended by ambassadors from the major countries of Europe. It was the last major Catholic ceremony in Scotland. Because it was a Catholic ceremony many of the Protestant nobles, and the English ambassador, chose not to attend the church ceremony. They waited outside the church door, but took a full part in the celebrations held afterwards. No expense was spared in the celebration banquet in Stirling

Castle's Great Hall, which can be visited today. Many courses of food and much wine were served. A major fight nearly broke out when some of Mary's French servants, dressed as satyrs and nymphs, taunted the English delegation by wiggling their tails at them. It must have been quite a party!

Mary's husband, Lord Darnley, was still being extremely difficult because Mary refused to declare him king and co-ruler. Darnley, in a great sulk, refused to attend the christening or celebrations. By now Mary was completely disillusioned with her husband, and for good reason. This once attractive young man had changed almost beyond recognition in two years into a loud-mouthed drunkard, who was serially promiscuous with women and possibly men too. He had been involved in the murder of Rizzio. He had not attended James' christening, a clear insult which questioned James' legitimacy and Mary's honour. If this was fiction it wouldn't be believed!

Was Darnley or Rizzio the Father of Mary's Child?

The arguments in favour of Rizzio being the father are:

- Mary was very close to Rizzio, and within months of the likely date of conception it was clear to everyone she was at odds with Darnley.
- Many people at the time thought this likely.
- Mary had spent her formative year in the licentious French court, where affairs were commonplace.
- James VI\I grew to 5 feet 2 inches and was rather ugly. Both Mary and Darnley were about 6 foot and good looking. There is conflicting evidence about the physical appearance of Rizzio, but it generally points to him being short and not particularly good looking, rather like James.
- Rizzio was intelligent, like James. Although Mary was intelligent, it seems unlikely that Darnley was.

The arguments against are that:

- The timing of the pregnancy makes it seem improbable. James was born on 15 June 1566. There is no evidence that he was premature, and therefore the likely month of conception was September 1565. At that time Darnley and Mary were involved together in the Chase-about raid.
- Mary treated her servants well and was liked by them, but she considered them well below her status.
- Mary's strong religious beliefs would argue against an affair, particularly so soon after her marriage, before she was totally disillusioned with Darnley.

In summary it is possible that Rizzio was the father, but it is very unlikely.

7. Exit Lord Darnley and Enter the Earl of Bothwell

Although Mary and Darnley's marriage had completely broken down, it would have been extremely difficult for Mary to get a divorce. And if Mary had divorced Darnley, in the legal system of the times her son would have become illegitimate, and therefore not able to inherit the crown.

It was during the three weeks that Mary was at Craigmillar that a group of senior nobles are believed to have met and agreed to murder Darnley. They agreed the "Craigmillar Bond", a pact to murder him. The lords detested Darnley. He had been involved in the murder of Rizzio but had soon after abandoned them and tried to re-ingratiate himself with Mary. The Lords considered Darnley overbearing, arrogant and completely untrustworthy. One of the many mysteries of Mary's reign is whether she was involved in the decision to murder her husband, whether she knew about it and turned a blind eye, or was entirely out of the picture.

In February 1567 Darnley was suffering from what is likely to have been syphilis, from one of his many dalliances with prostitutes. He had been recuperating in his family estates in the west of Scotland. Mary had visited him there, and persuaded him to come back to Edinburgh, something that was to be used against her in view of subsequent events. Mary wanted Darnley to stay at Craigmillar Castle. But Darnley was concerned about being under the roof of one of Mary's strongest supporters, Simon Preston of Craigmillar. Therefore he chose instead to lodge in Kirk o' Fields, a lodging on what was then the outskirts of Edinburgh, receiving treatment. He was covered in what were probably syphilitic sores, from his dalliances with prostitutes, and emotionally out of control. The young man, who only two years before had been healthy and attractive, was now incapacitated and pox ridden.

On 9 February 1567 Mary visited Lord Darnley at Kirk o' Fields, but left to attend the wedding celebration of two of her servants. This was to be construed by her critics as further proof that she was involved in what followed.

In the middle of the night a tremendous explosion was heard in Edinburgh. Darnley's lodgings in Kirk o' Fields had been destroyed by the blast. Darnley's body, and the body of a servant were found in the garden outside. Both had been strangled. They had presumably heard their murderers preparing to set off the explosives, and had escaped from the house into the garden. Their killers had strangled them there. Kirk o' Field no longer exists (it was blown up after all), but it was part of the Church of St Mary in the Fields, and was sited near the corner of the Pleasance and Brown Street

Mary then acted foolishly. In a deeply religious country she should have gone into formal mourning after the death of her husband. Even if she did not feel like mourning someone she detested, it was not appropriate to continue with normal activities. That she did not go into mourning was taken by her detractors as a sign of her involvement and guilt.

Whilst historians still debate if Mary had been complicit in the murder, much of the Edinburgh mob certainly thought she had been. Scurrilous posters began to appear showing a topless mermaid (signifying a prostitute), which would have been understood to represent Mary. Beside the mermaid on the poster was a hare, which was Bothwell's family emblem. The message was clear. Mary was little better than a prostitute and linked to Bothwell. Rumour was rife. The young queen who had come back to Scotland with so much hope and public support was now held in contempt by much of the population.

Edinburgh was in ferment. Bothwell was tried for Darnley's murder, but he arranged for several thousand of his followers to come into Edinburgh, and the court was duly intimidated into acquitting him.

Bothwell was a ruffian with great ambitions. He managed, whether by threat or bribery, to get 29 lords or bishops to sign a bond supporting his acquittal of the charge of murdering Darnley. The bond also stated that Bothwell was an appropriate suitor to marry the queen, and that they would support him if he did so. The bond is known as the Ainslie Tavern Bond. It seems likely that the conspirators met in a tavern run by a man named Ainslie, although the tavern has never been identified.

In April 1567 Mary visited Stirling where her ten month old son was staying in the royal nursery, under the protection of the trustworthy John Erskine, Earl of Mar. The young queen spent a day playing with her child, which must have been great pleasure and comfort to her.

Mary didn't know it, but this was to be the last time she was to see her son. Mar refused to let her take him to Edinburgh. Mar, as guardian of the child, was worried about the child's safety in the frenzied atmosphere of Edinburgh, where he could have been kidnapped or worse. It was a wise decision on his part.

Mary's life was to get even more difficult and bizarre. On the return journey to Edinburgh her party was waylaid by Bothwell, supported by a large band of his ruffians. Mary was abducted by Bothwell and taken to Dunbar Castle, where according to some contemporary sources he raped her. It is possible that the abduction was pre-arranged between Mary and Bothwell, yet another imponderable in Mary's life.

Mary's life now began to spin completely out of control. Less than four weeks after the abduction, and three months after Darnley was murdered, Mary married Bothwell in a sparsely attended Protestant ceremony in the Palace of Holyroodhouse. Only weeks before the marriage Bothwell had arranged a divorce from his wife of a year, citing his adultery with her maid! Mary's marriage to Bothwell resulted in her alienating much of Scotland. It was an incredibly stupid thing to do. I can only think that she entered into it because she was very frightened, enamoured with Bothwell and undergoing some sort of a nervous breakdown.

Bothwell, like Darnley before him, was arrogant and overbearing, although Bothwell was at least courageous. Soon a group of Lords, known as the Confederate Lords, were scheming to overthrow Bothwell and Mary. Many of the nobles now conspiring against Bothwell had signed the Ainslie Tavern Bond supporting him. Such was the fickleness of the nobles' loyalties. Their outward message was that they planned to "rescue" Mary from Bothwell, but their intentions were clear.

Bothwell and Mary began putting together a small army. But they felt at risk in Holyroodhouse, and decided to decamp to Borthwick Castle. Borthwick is a massive tower house twelve miles south of Edinburgh, and looks in some ways like Hermitage Castle. As troops of the Confederate Lords began to converge on the castle Bothwell escaped to try to muster his men, leaving Mary in the castle. She escaped the next day. Mary was lowered from a window dressed as a page boy, so she could make her way on foot through the encircling forces without being recognised, and join up with Bothwell.

Mary and Bothwell then gathered together their supporters, and met the Confederate Lords' forces at Carberry Hill, near Musselburgh, east of Edinburgh. The "battle" of Carberry Hill was something of a stand-off. Both armies were of roughly equal size, but when lined up against each other it became clear that neither had any real desire to fight and kill their countrymen. Mary's troops began to desert. Mary as well was indecisive, and decided to negotiate with the Confederate Lords rather than risk a battle which would have resulted in significant bloodshed. In the end she agreed to surrender providing Bothwell was allowed to go free.

James Douglas, Earl of Morton, and the Dangers in Being Regent

The Earl of Morton was to be convicted of Darnley's murder, but not until 1581, fourteen years after the event. Morton was executed by the maiden, an early guillotine, which he himself had introduced to Scotland in 1564. The maiden was used in the execution of more than 150 people, and can be seen in the National Museum of Scotland in Edinburgh. The maiden was a non-discriminatory device. Its victims included minor criminals and miscreants, up to the Earl of Morton and the Marquess of Argyll.

It is likely that the Earl of Morton was a ringleader in the plot, but there is no conclusive proof. The conviction provided an excuse for James VI, Mary and Darnley's son, to have Morton executed. Morton had acted as regent, ruling Scotland on behalf of the young James VI, but had fallen out of favour. James may also have felt that the conviction shifted blame for his father's murder from his mother.

There were four regents during James's minority. The Earl of Moray was assassinated in 1570. The Earl of Lennox died in a skirmish with forces supporting Mary in 1571. The Earl of Mar, the guardian of Mary's son in Stirling Castle, died in 1572 probably of natural causes. But some people believe he was poisoned by the Earl of Morton, so Morton could become Regent.

Being Regent was a very sought after role, but this writer would turn it down!

8. The End Game in Scotland

Imprisonment in Lochleven Castle

Mary had expected to be treated with respect by the Confederate Lords, but it was not to be. The Lords took her back to Edinburgh, where she was greeted by jeering crowds, rather than the cheering crowds she had hoped for. Darnley's murder, her suspected involvement in it, and her marriage only three months later to Lord Bothwell, a key suspect, played a major part in turning a large part of the population against her.

From Edinburgh she was taken to Lochleven Castle, strategically sited on an island in Loch (Lake) Leven, about half way between Edinburgh and Perth. The Confederate Lords no doubt thought that imprisoning Mary in a castle on an island in the middle of a loch would have ensured she was under their control, without hope of escape or rescue.

Lochleven Castle was the home of Sir William Douglas of Lochleven. This was to be Mary's prison for the next eleven months, from June 1567 to May 1568, and Sir William Douglas her gaoler. It was a reasonably comfortable prison though, and Mary had two ladies-in-waiting in attendance, and a doctor as she was initially pregnant by Bothwell, and not in good health for much of her imprisonment.

Mary already knew Lochleven castle quite well. In 1563 she had confronted John Knox, the firebrand Scottish minister, there. Knox vehemently objected to Mary retaining her Catholic faith. Mary had hoped to charm him, but her efforts were of no avail. Amongst his many complaints against Mary he objected to female rulers. Knox didn't budge from his

Lochleven Castle on an island in Loch Leven.

extreme anti-Catholic and misogynistic views.

Mary was pregnant with twins by the Earl of Bothwell, but at about three months term, and around four weeks after arriving at Lochleven she had a miscarriage. She was in a depressed and vulnerable state following all that had happened, including her miscarriage. The Lords threatened to murder her and so forced her to abdicate in favour of her infant son James.

James was crowned James VI of Scotland when he was thirteen months old in a Protestant ceremony at the Church of the Holy Rude in Stirling, two hundred yards or so outside the castle. The Church of the Holy Rude was a plain Protestant church, unlike the elaborately decorated Chapel Royal in the castle, which was associated with Catholic ceremonies.

The ceremony was sparsely attended and performed quickly by the usually bombastic and verbose John Knox. There was a concern that Mary's largely Catholic supporters in Stirling and the surrounding areas might riot, and therefore the nobles attending the ceremony wanted to return to the safety of Stirling Castle as quickly as possible.

As time passed Mary started to recover, and the legendary Stuart charm returned to this still beautiful twenty-four year old woman. The owner of the castle, Mary's gaoler Sir William Douglas, had a younger brother George. They also had a young relation, Willie Douglas, living with them. Willie's parents had died and therefore he was in their care. Soon Mary had charmed George and Willie, and they were intent on helping her to escape.

In order to escape Mary had to get across the loch. Mary's first attempt, disguised as a laundry woman, was unsuccessful. Her disguise did not fool the castle boatman. A beautiful, very tall young woman speaking with a French accent could never pass for anyone but the Queen of Scots.

On 2 May 1568 they made a second attempt. Lady Douglas, the wife of Sir William, had given birth and the garrison was preoccupied with celebrating this, rather than guarding Mary. As Sir William Douglas was eating and no doubt a little drunk, young Willie Douglas managed to steal the castle keys. Meanwhile Mary changed into old clothes, and made her way down to the landing stage via a postern gate (a small secondary gate). Then together with Willie and a servant woman they made their way by boat across the loch. Meanwhile one of Mary's ladies-in-waiting dressed in Mary's clothes, and made sure she was seen from a distance, so it appeared that Mary was still in the castle.

Once Mary and her party reached the shore, as prearranged a group of her supporters, including George Douglas, were waiting with horses to help her leave the area. Mary spent her first night of freedom in Niddry Castle (now a private home), about seven miles from Linlithgow. She then rode to the territory of the Hamilton family in west central Scotland. They were likely to support her as they were rivals and enemies of Darnley's family. They also aspired to control Scotland by having control of the queen, or by marrying her into their family.

67

The Battle of Langside

Before many days had passed the story of Mary's dramatic escape was known through much of Scotland, and supporters were rallying to her colours. Supporters flocked to her side, not just Catholics, but Protestants who strongly believed in the hereditary right of monarchy, and that she was the rightful monarch. These weren't just the common people; nine Lords and nine bishops also joined her ranks.

Mary's intention was to get to Dumbarton Castle, where she could be reinforced from France if France was prepared to help her. Dumbarton Castle was a strong castle on the Firth of Clyde (the estuary of the River Clyde), west of Glasgow, from where Mary had sailed to France as a child. The Confederate Lords also mobilised their forces under the Earl of Moray, Mary's half-brother, who was acting as regent for Mary's infant son.

Mary's and Moray's armies met in battle on 13 May 1568 at Langside, now a Glasgow suburb but then a small village south of Glasgow. Mary's forces, although at 6,000 men significantly larger than the 4,000 men of the Confederate Lords, were badly led by the less than competent Earl of Argyll. Moray's arquebusiers (soldiers armed with an early form of rifle) quickly established themselves in the village, led by Kirkcaldy of Grange, an experienced and competent soldier. To try to dislodge them Mary's cavalry charged along Langside's single street into the arquebusiers' fire, not a winning strategy.

After heavy fighting Mary's troops were beaten, but not decisively so. The Earl of Moray ordered his cavalry not to harry Mary's forces as they retreated, and so reduced the bloodshed. Mary could have regrouped and fought another day if she wished. Whether Mary panicked or just didn't want further bloodshed we shall never know, but she decided to retreat and leave Scotland.

Langside is a busy Glasgow suburb now, with nothing remaining from 1568. In 1887 a monument was erected to commemorate the battle, and a number of local streets have names reminiscent of the battle, such as Battlefield Road.

How Scotland's history might have been different if instead of losing, Mary had decisively won the battle.

Young George Douglas, who had helped Mary escape from Lochleven Castle, was faithful to the end. This picture, from the Library of Congress image library, shows Mary comforting the dying George at the Battle of Langside.

The Battle of Langside memorial in a busy road junction in Langside, now part of Glasgow.

9. Mary's Last Night in Scotland

Mary and a small party of twenty supporters spent an uncomfortable two days travelling the ninety miles to south west Scotland. Mary cut off her long auburn hair to reduce the possibility of being recognised. But this was a forlorn hope. A young woman of nearly six feet, speaking with a French accent and protected by a party of twenty supporters could only be the queen fleeing after the defeat at Langside.

Mary spent her last night in Scotland in Dundrennan Abbey, south of Kirkcudbright and only a mile from the sea at the Solway Firth. Dundrennan is now a ruin, but it had been a major Cistercian Abbey. Historic Scotland consider the north and south transepts to be the best preserved late 12th century Cistercian architecture in Scotland. As Scotland had become officially Protestant eight years before in 1560, Dundrennan's days were numbered and it would have been in decline when Mary arrived. In time the Abbey was used as a source of stone for buildings in the village of Dundrennan.

Many of her counsellors advised her to go to France, but against their advice Mary decided to seek sanctuary with her cousin Queen Elizabeth in England. She hoped Elizabeth would help her reclaim her crown.

On 16 May 1568 she left Scotland with twenty followers in a fishing boat from Abbey Burnfoot, the Abbey's small harbour on the Solway Firth. Abbey Burnfoot is about a mile and a half from the Abbey itself. Her destination was Workington in

The remains of Dundrennan Abbey.

Cumbria, a four hour crossing of the firth. She had already written to Elizabeth's representative in Cumbria's capital Carlisle, asking for sanctuary.

Mary had arrived in Scotland as queen in 1561, aged only eighteen, travelling in a royal galley in great splendour. She had been warmly welcomed and acclaimed by most of her subjects. She left only six years nine months later, exhausted and terrified, shorn of her once beautiful auburn hair. Instead of a royal galley she travelled in a small fishing boat. No doubt she smelled strongly of fish.

10. Mary's Life After Leaving Scotland

Mary had intended her escape to England to be a temporary measure. She had hoped her cousin Elizabeth would provide her with support to regain her throne. But instead Elizabeth decided to hold her under "house arrest". Elizabeth and her advisors were frightened that a Catholic queen with a strong claim to the English throne could become a focus for a Catholic rebellion in England. And very foolishly Mary had never formally relinquished her claim to the English crown, made only ten years before when she was in France and under the influence of her Guise relatives.

Therefore Mary presented a very real threat to Elizabeth. And if Mary was to return to Scotland and regain the crown, it was not in Elizabeth's best interests to have a Catholic, pro-French monarch ruling Scotland. Mary's half-brother Lord James Stuart was acting as regent on behalf of Mary's son and was proving to be very pro-English. It was therefore in Elizabeth's interest that he continued to rule Scotland.

Mary was often held in some comfort, and allowed to retain her servants, but she was never allowed freedom. She was moved from castle to castle, never near the coast or close to England's remaining Catholic heartlands, so rescue would have been very difficult.

In April 1570 Pope Pius excommunicated Elizabeth, which made her a legitimate target for extremist Catholics. Therefore during Mary's time in captivity there were a number of plots against Elizabeth's life, some of which Mary would have been aware of.

At one point Mary and the Duke of Norfolk, a cousin of Queen Elizabeth and the head of one of England's leading and wealthiest Catholic families, discussed marriage. They had only met once, but they exchanged love letters. Mary obviously saw this as a way to obtain her freedom.

When Elizabeth became aware of this, she was very angry. She saw the possible marriage of the Queen of Scots who had a claim on the English throne to England's wealthiest landowner as a major threat. This resulted in Norfolk being imprisoned in the Tower of London. When he was released he became involved in the Ridolfi plot, a plot to land Spanish troops in England who would support a Catholic uprising. Elizabeth would have been deposed, and Mary released to marry Norfolk and to rule England as a Catholic queen. When this plot was revealed by an informer, Norfolk was given a one day trial followed by his execution.

Mary's life continued as a captive. After nineteen years in captivity Mary became increasingly desperate, and fell for a plot orchestrated by Elizabeth's spymaster, Francis Walsingham, to entrap her. Francis Walsingham was very anti-Catholic. He had been English ambassador in Paris during the St Bartholomew day massacre, when Catholics rose up and murdered thousands of Protestant men, women and children. Walsingham had witnessed this, and had felt his and his family's life to be at risk. Therefore he was prepared to stop at nothing to ensure Catholics did not come to power in England. So without Elizabeth's knowledge Walsingham devised a plot to entrap Mary.

Partly encouraged by Walsingham's agents, a group of young Catholic noblemen led by the 24 year old Antony Babington conspired to murder Elizabeth and raise a Catholic revolution, which they believed would be supported by Spanish troops. Mary took Walsingham's bait, and attempted to conspire with Babington and Catholic nobles in England against Elizabeth.

Mary was in much closer confinement than earlier in her captivity. She was despairing, having been in captivity for 19 years, and was prepared to attempt anything to obtain her freedom. Mary was communicating with her supporters via encrypted messages in a water-tight container placed in barrels of beer. Because of the risk of infection being passed in drinking water, before clean water was available large quantities of low alcohol beer was consumed instead of water. The alcohol killed the germs.

Unfortunately for Mary, Walsingham's staff were aware of this process, and were routinely intercepting the messages. They understood the cyphers used. They therefore knew Mary was supporting the plot. So they gained the evidence necessary to show Mary's involvement.

After a trial in which Mary was found guilty of conspiring against Elizabeth, on 1 February 1587 Elizabeth signed Mary's death warrant. Her advisors had the death warrant rushed to Fotheringhay Castle where Mary was being held. They saw Mary as a real focus for Catholic resentment against Elizabeth, and therefore a major danger to the Protestant religion in England. Elizabeth's advisors wanted Mary executed before Elizabeth could change her mind.

On 8 February 1587 Mary, then aged 44, was beheaded at Fotheringhay Castle. She died bravely, in front of a crowd of up to 300 people in the castle's great hall, after saying prayers in the Catholic manner. Mary was as true to her religion at the end as she had been throughout her life. When she removed her outer garment before the executioner's axe fell she revealed a petticoat of scarlet, the colour signifying martyrdom in the Catholic church.

Two rather gruesome incidents occurred immediately after the execution. The executioner tried to lift Mary's head aloft by the hair. But Mary had aged, and he found that he was holding a wig, as the head, covered in rather sparse grey hair, rolled away. At the same time Mary's little terrier, which had been hiding under her voluminous skirts rushed out, and became covered in Mary's blood.

The scant remains of Fotheringhay Castle. The castle was an old motte and bailey type castle. It is in a very attractive setting in the village of Fotheringhay beside the River Nene, about ten miles west of Peterborough. Almost all the masonry has been removed, but the earthworks of ditch, bailey and motte are very clearly recognisable. Rather appropriately the motte is covered in thistles.

Elizabeth was to claim that although she had of course signed Mary's death warrant, it had been dispatched by her secretary and the execution carried out without her authority. This was probably a charade, in an attempt to shift responsibility from her. She had just had a strongly Catholic former Queen of Scots and Dowager Queen Consort of France executed. The possibility of Catholic Europe starting a war to avenge Mary was high. Elizabeth wanted to distance herself from the execution as far as possible. Davison her secretary was to spend some time imprisoned in the tower for issuing the death warrant, before being released.

Elizabeth's attempts to distance herself from the execution didn't work. We met Prince Philip of Spain in chapter 3 when he married Elizabeth's half-sister Queen Mary, or Bloody Mary as she became known. Now as King Philip II of Spain he was to use the execution of Mary Queen of Scots as part of his justification for unleashing the Spanish Armada in an unsuccessful attempt to invade England. The Armada sailed only a year after Mary's execution. The King of Spain who directed the Spanish Armada had married Mary Tudor, the then Queen of England, when he was a prince! Facts can be stranger than fiction.

Mary was buried in Peterborough Cathedral, which is near to Fotheringhay Castle. When her son, James VI of Scotland assumed the English crown as James I after Elizabeth's death, he had Mary's body exhumed and interred in the Lady Chapel in Westminster Abbey. Westminster Abbey is England's most prestigious royal mausoleum. Many major churches have Lady Chapels, the lady being the Virgin Mary. Mary's cousin, sometimes friend (although they never met), and eventual nemesis Queen Elizabeth is interred in a room on one side of the chapel, and Mary on the other side. Unfortunately taking photographs in the Abbey is not allowed.

The Countess of Lennox (formerly Lady Margaret Douglas), Darnley's mother, is in a smaller tomb in the same side-room as Mary. The Countess had originally considered Mary responsible for the death of her son. However Mary's supporters cobbled together a counterfeit "deathbed" confession from Bothwell, designed to emphasise Mary's innocence in the murder. The Countess was taken in by this, and she then wrote to Mary in very friendly terms. This is just as well; had she felt Mary was implicated in the murder of her son, they could hardly rest in peace together!

And What Happened to the Earl of Bothwell?

After escaping from the field at the abortive battle of Carberry Hill, whilst Mary was imprisoned in Lochleven Castle Bothwell escaped by boat towards the Orkneys, pursued by a soldier, Kirkcaldy of Grange. After a sea battle in the Orkneys, he made his way to Norway, where he had lived before. But Bothwell had a problematic history in Norway. He had deserted a former mistress from a noble Norwegian family, and had various creditors.

Bothwell was handed over to the King of Denmark, who also ruled Norway at the time. The King of Denmark saw Bothwell, the husband of the Queen of Scots, as a potential political bargaining chip, and Bothwell was held in captivity. However, with Mary imprisoned in England Bothwell's usefulness as a possible bargaining chip declined, and he was held in increasing squalor. After ten years he died, some historians believe insane and chained to a pillar, in Dragsholm Castle in Denmark.

11. Mary and Her Legacy

What Was Mary Really Like?

Mary as a child was vivacious and friendly, captivating most people she came in contact with. Henri II of France, her future father-in-law, described her as "the most perfect child". In Henri II's court in France she was given precedence over the French princesses since she was the Queen of Scotland and intended as the queen consort of France. Her position bred in her a strong sense of her entitlement. She was a pretty child who grew to be a good-looking woman, with a pale complexion and auburn hair. At almost six feet tall and always well dressed, she was strikingly attractive.

Mary was well educated in France, speaking a number of languages, as well as being proficient in the traditional aristocratic female skills of the time of dancing, music, needlework and embroidery. But while she was educated in the skills required to be a queen consort of France, she wasn't educated in those required to assume personal rule as queen in the bear-pit of Scottish politics.

As an adult she had considerable charm, which she used to good effect. When held prisoner in Lochleven Castle the 25 year old woman charmed the young Douglases into helping her escape. After the murder of Rizzio she won Darnley over.

Her charm had fatal consequences for one of her servants, the young French poet Chastelard. Chastelard lost his head over her (literally). Chastelard was a member of Mary's court, and became infatuated with her. One night he hid under her bed. For this he was banished from court. The following night the foolish youth burst into Mary's bedroom when she was undressing, saying he wanted to explain himself. For this he was beheaded.

In modern parlance Mary was also sporty as well as traditionally feminine. She was a good horsewoman, and scandalised some of her more conservative advisors by wearing breeches when playing real tennis at Falkland Palace.

She was almost certainly naïve and foolish, allowing passion to rule her decision making too often. Passion prevented her seeing Darnley's manifest faults, and she married him far too quickly. Likewise with Bothwell, although I suspect she was nearing complete nervous collapse by the time she married him, so rational judgement was out of the question.

In addition to the personal errors noted in the previous paragraphs, Mary made some major political misjudgements. Her Catholic religion caused considerable friction with key members of the Scottish nobility. It would have been easier to have become Protestant, but she just couldn't forgo the religion she believed in. She could however have been more discrete about it, and to have had fewer foreign Catholics in her entourage, which bred suspicion and anger amongst the Scottish Protestants. Another mistake was not relinquishing all claims to the English throne while Elizabeth was alive. Because of Mary's claim, Elizabeth saw her as a potential enemy. Yet Mary was naïve enough to trust her, based on their usually friendly correspondence.

I have great sympathy for Mary. She was only eighteen when she assumed personal rule in Scotland, having little previous knowledge of the country or the nobility. She also had to deal with what was at that time a fanatical and intolerant version of the Protestant religion. This was a reaction against the Catholicism of the time, and is very different from the tolerant and compassionate Church of Scotland of today. Ruling Scotland in the 1560s would have been a challenge for Machiavelli, and her religious faith and gender, together with her political inexperience, made it an unsurmountable challenge.

Mary's Legacy

Mary's flight from Scotland did not end the civil war that had developed between her supporters and the Confederate Lords. The Earl of Moray who ruled Scotland on behalf of Mary's son James, was assassinated by one of Mary's supporters in 1570. Her supporters held Edinburgh Castle until 1573, when they were forced to surrender by English artillery, brought in at the request of the Scottish government.

What about Mary's father, James V's prophesy on his deathbed which we mentioned earlier: "It came wi' a lass, it will go we' a lass". He was right in implying that Mary would not be able to successfully rule Scotland, but not that the Stuart dynasty would end with her.

Mary's legacy was her son James, who she was forced to abdicate in favour of when he was only thirteen months old. Mary was never to see him again, although they corresponded when she was in captivity. James's support for his mother was lukewarm, as he did not want to antagonise Elizabeth I or key English Protestants, and so lessen his chance of inheriting the English crown on the death of the childless Elizabeth. James achieved his ambition. James VI of Scotland became James I of England in 1603 after Elizabeth died from natural causes. James's descendants included Charles I and II, and the British royal family to this day have Stuart blood in their veins.

Kong James showed some regret for not supporting his mother while she was held prisoner by Elizabeth. After James became King of England, Fotheringhay Castle, where she had been executed, was allowed to fall into ruin and was then dismantled. In 1612 James instructed that Mary's remains be moved from Peterborough Cathedral to Westminster Abbey, to a tomb that was bigger than Elizabeth's. A copy of part of the tomb is in the National Museum of Scotland in Edinburgh.

Mary had stressed the need for religious tolerance, but having a Catholic monarch ruling Scotland had made a restoration of

Catholicism as the state religion of Scotland a possibility. Mary's flight in 1568, and the absence of support for her from Elizabeth I put an end to any possibility of Catholicism being restored in Scotland, although it was another five years before hostilities, known as the Marian Civil War, ended. Dumbarton Castle held out for her until 1571, and Edinburgh Castle until 1573.

But with Mary a prisoner in England from 1568 the Scottish Reformation was secure, and a closer relationship between Protestant Scotland and Protestant England possible. Had Scotland become Catholic, for good or bad Scottish and British history could have been very different. And as Britain was to have a major impact on the world, world history too might have been different.

12. Edinburgh - National Museum of Scotland

Chambers Street,
Edinburgh,
EH1 1JF

> Contains several exhibits relating to Mary. Scotland's premier museum.

When in Edinburgh, visit the National Museum of Scotland in Chambers Street. Whilst exhibitions can change, in relation to Mary you are likely to see:

- A cast of Mary's tomb. Mary's tomb is in Westminster Abbey in London. Her son James VI of Scotland (James I of England), had an impressive tomb built for her many years after her execution, probably out of guilt for having done nothing to help her when she was held captive by Elizabeth I.

- A silver coin minted in Mary's time, showing her and her husband Henry, Lord Darnley with Darnley's name before Mary. These were quickly withdrawn from circulation as the marriage soured, and replaced by a coin with Mary's name first, which is also on display.

- Various items of jewellery, such as the Penicuik jewels, and a locket and silver crucifix, believed to have belonged to Mary.

- And one other gruesome exhibit, the Maiden, an early guillotine, used to execute the 4th Earl of Morton for his alleged involvement in the murder of Lord Darnley.

The National Museum is a fantastic resource for anyone interested in Scottish history. You will be enthralled and end up spending many hours there! There are also informative free guided tours.

Mary's tomb is in Westminster Abbey, but a cast of the tomb is available for all to see in the National Museum of Scotland.

Appendix 1 - Mary's Timeline

The following table summarises Mary's eventful life. Many of the main Scottish heritage landmarks associated with her are highlighted in bold, and are described in appendix 2.

1542	8 December	Mary is born in **Linlithgow Palace**
	14 December	Mary's father, James V dies, leaving her Queen of Scotland
1543		Mary is sent to **Stirling Castle** for her safety. The Treaty of Greenwich is signed, contracting Mary to marry Henry VIII's son Edward when she is of age.
1544		The Scots renege on the Treaty of Greenwich. Henry VIII troops rampage through southern Scotland, to terrorise the Scots into complying with the treaty.
1547	September	Mary is sent to **Inchmahome Priory** for her safety. There was a large English army in Scotland, and her guardians did not want her trapped in Stirling Castle.
1548	August	Mary, aged 5 years 8 months is sent from **Dumbarton Castle** to live in France, contracted to marry the Dauphin (the heir to the French crown).

1560		After years of discord, Scotland becomes officially Protestant, although a large Catholic minority still exists. The North and Dumfries and Galloway remain largely Catholic.
1548-1561		Mary grows up in France and marries the Dauphin on 24 April 1558. She becomes queen consort of France from the death of Henri II on 10 July 1559. After 18 months as queen of France, Mary's husband dies.
1561	19 August	Mary returns to Scotland to begin her personal reign as queen. Her main residence is the **Palace of Holyroodhouse.**
1561-1565		Marys reign proceeds reasonably well. She puts down two rebellions, one a Catholic and one a Protestant.
1565	29 July	Mary marries Lord Darnley. Whilst a superficially attractive young man, in fact he is a dissolute, weak, sexually licentious drunkard. Mary soon realises her mistake.
1566	9 March	Mary's secretary Rizzio has enraged the nobles. He is murdered in Mary's apartment in the **Palace of Holyroodhouse** by a group of nobles that include her husband Lord Darnley.
	19 June	Mary gives birth to the future James VI in the security of **Edinburgh Castle**.

1567	9 February	Lord Darnley is murdered. Lord Bothwell leads the nobles involved in the murder, and Mary may be implicated. Everything begins to fall apart for Mary
	15 May	Mary marries Lord Bothwell. An appalling decision.
	15 June	Many nobles have turned against Mary. She surrenders to them at Carberry Hill rather than fight, and shortly afterwards is imprisoned in **Lochleven Castle**.
	24 July	Mary is forced to abdicate on threat of death.
	29 July	Mary and Darnley's thirteen month old son is crowned James VI.
1568	2 May	Mary escapes from **Lochleven Castle**, and an army of her supporters gather.
	13 May	Mary loses the battle of **Langside**. She is now a fugitive.
	16 May	Mary leaves Scotland, having spent her last ever night on Scottish soil at **Dundrennan Abbey**.
1568-1587		Mary is held under house arrest in England, a captive of Elizabeth I, who fears that Mary may become a focus for a Catholic rebellion in England.
1587	8 February	After eighteen and a half years in captivity Mary is executed at Fotheringhay Castle.

Appendix 2 - The Main Scottish Sites Associated with Mary

A guide for anyone wanting to explore the main Scottish sites associated with Mary, either in person, or from an armchair!

Most of the sites are numbered in the chronological order that they first played a significant part in Mary's life.

Summary of the Sites

As indicated most are HES (Historic Environment Scotland, often shortened to Historic Scotland), properties.

1. Linlithgow Palace. Mary was born here in 1542 in what was a beautiful palace. Though now ruined, it is a beautiful ruin. (HES).

2. Stirling Castle. This was Mary's mother's main home. As a child she was largely brought up here for safety, as Henry VIII's troops terrorised Scotland, to try to force her marriage to Henry's son Edward. (HES).

3. Inchmahome Priory. Mary was sent here for three weeks as a child for her safety, whilst English troops ravaged Scotland. (HES).

4. Dumbarton Castle. At five years seven months Mary stayed here before leaving in a French fleet to be brought up in the safety of France. (HES).

5. Edinburgh - Palace of Holyroodhouse. Mary's main residence when she returned to Scotland in 1561 to rule as queen. Mary's apartment, where David Rizzio was murdered in 1566, is still here and open to tourists. It is largely as it was in her time. Still a royal residence in Scotland. For much of the year it is open to visitors, subject to an admission charge.

6. Edinburgh Castle. The castle dominates Edinburgh and is where Mary gave birth to the future James VI of Scotland, who later became James I of England. (HES).

7. Edinburgh - Craigmillar Castle. Mary was friendly with the Preston family who owned the castle and visited often. She spent some time here when she was suffering from depression after the birth of her child. (HES).

8. Edinburgh - National Museum of Scotland. When in Edinburgh this is a "must-see" site. It contains many artefacts relating to Mary's time. Scotland's premier museum.

9. Falkland Palace. A pleasure palace for the monarch of Scotland. Mary played tennis here in breeches, causing something of a scandal.

10. Dunfermline Abbey and Palace. Mary stayed here often when travelling to Fife and the north. (HES).

11. Mary Queen of Scots' House, Jedburgh. Mary may have stayed here when touring the Borders in 1566, presiding over a circuit court dispensing justice. Now an excellent museum dedicated to Mary's life.

12. Hermitage Castle. Mary visited her paramour and later husband Lord Bothwell, in this grim border castle. (HES).

13. Borthwick Castle. Mary made a daring escape from here dressed as a page boy.

14. Lochleven Castle. Mary's prison for almost a year in Scotland. Here she was forced to abdicate in favour of her baby son, before making a daring escape. (HES).

15. Langside. The site of a major battle, on 13 May 1568. Mary's forces lost, and Mary left Scotland forever. Now a busy suburb of Glasgow, but worth visiting because it is so pivotal to Mary's story.

16. Dundrennan Abbey. Mary spent her last night in Scotland in this once beautiful Border abbey on 15 May 1568, before leaving Scotland forever on 16 May. (HES).

17. St Andrews. This was the spiritual heart of Scotland during the Catholic period, and Mary visited several times. It has many connections to the Scottish Reformation. It is a very attractive town, with much for the history fan to see. (The key sites of the castle and cathedral ruins are managed by HES.)

Visiting the Sites

All the buildings and sites in the book are located in the Fife, Scottish Lowlands and the Scottish border area. It should be possible to visit them all in about two weeks. These are amongst the most important historic buildings in Scotland, and therefore provide an excellent introduction to Scottish history in general, and not just to Mary's story.

The majority of the buildings are now in the care of Historic Environment Scotland (HES). All of the HES sites are open to the public, although many are shut, or have restricted hours, in winter. Any visitor intending to visit many of the sites should consider buying an annual membership to Historic Environment Scotland (HES), or at least an Explorer Pass which allows access to their sites for a limited period. Opening times, ticket prices, membership details and further details of these sites can be obtained from their website:

https://www.historicenvironment.scot

The following sites are not in the care of HES:

> **Borthwick Castle** is run as a venue for weddings and corporate events. Https://www.borthwickcastle.com
>
> The **National Museum of Scotland** is of course a public museum.
>
> **Falkland Palace** is managed by the National Trust for Scotland. There is an entry charge. The website is:
> https://www.nts.org.uk/
>
> **Mary Queen of Scots' House** is in Jedburgh. Entry to this excellent museum is free. The website is:
> http://www.jedburgh.org.uk/attraction-mary-queen-of-scots-house.

The **Palace of Holyroodhouse** is not an HES site. There is a charge to visit the Palace. Its website is:

https://www.royalcollection.org.uk/visit/palace-of-holyroodhouse.

Travelling to the Sites

If you want to travel to the sites using public transport, www.travelinescotland.com is an excellent website for planning your journey, and also shows ticket prices. Traveline Scotland also has iOS and Android apps. Google maps also has a useful public transport option.

Within Edinburgh the Lothian Buses app for Android and iOS is excellent, and will help you to plan a visit by bus to Edinburgh Castle, Holyroodhouse, the National Museum of Scotland and Craigmillar Castle.

A visitor with limited time or restricted to public transport may wish to concentrate on visiting the four Edinburgh sites noted above, together with Stirling Castle and Linlithgow Palace. All are major sites in Mary's story, and are easy to travel to by public transport.

Dundrennan Abbey is difficult (but not impossible) to get to by public transport, and therefore it may be best to omit it if you don't have your own transport. Likewise Hermitage Castle and Inchmahome Priory are difficult to get to if you don't have a car. If you do travel to Dundrennan though there are a range of other HES sites well worth visiting within travelling distance, although without a Mary association. For example Caerlaverock, Threave and McLellan Castles, and Sweetheart Abbey. McLellan Castle is in the nearby town of Kirkcudbright, and the town is also very attractive.

Appendix 3 - Further Reading

It is likely that many hundreds of books have been written about Mary, and therefore this is not a comprehensive bibliography! However of the books I have read, I would particularly recommend the following.

Fraser, Antonia, *Mary Queen of Scots,* London, Weidenfeld and Nicolson, 1969.

Graham, Roderick, An Accidental Tragedy – The Life of Mary Queen of Scots, Edinburgh, Birlinn, 2012.

Guy, John, My Heart is My Own: The Life of Mary Queen of Scots, New York, Harper 2004.

Porter, Linda, *Crown of Thistles: The Fatal Inheritance of Mary Queen of Scots*, London, Pan, 2013. Covers Mary's Stewart ancestors, as well as Mary.

Weir, Alison, Mary Queen of Scots and the Murder of Lord Darnley, London, Vintage, 2008.

For readers wanting something "lighter" than the above, but nonetheless informative, I recommend:

Mayhew, Mickey, *The Little Book of Mary Queen of Scots*, Stroud, The History Press, 2015.

Mickey Mayhew's book is a good starting point to this complex life story.

Two further books trace Mary's travels:

Burnet, Andrew; Scott, Nicki; Gall, Sally; *Mary Was Here: Where Mary Queen of Scots Went and What She Did There,* Historic Environment Scotland 2013.

Just as I was finalising *Mary Queen of Scots' Scotland*, I became aware of:

Calley, Roy. *On the Trail of Mary, Queen of Scots,* Amberley Publishing, 2017. This book traces Mary through Scotland, France and England.

Anyone wanting to learn more about Mary's interesting mother, Marie of Guise, should read:

Clegg, Melanie, Scourge of Henry VIII: The Life of Marie De Guise, Pen and Sword History, 2016.

Marshall, Rosalind K, *Mary of Guise Queen of Scots*, Edinburgh, NMS Enterprises Ltd – Publishing, 2001.

Reading about Mary's life can provide an excellent introduction to 16th century Scottish history for children. I recommend:

Douglas, Elizabeth, *Mary Queen of Scots*, Edinburgh, NMS Enterprises Ltd – Publishing, 2000.

Dear Reader,

This book is intended to be an introduction to Mary's life, and particularly her life in Scotland and the Scotland that Mary knew. If you have enjoyed it and found it informative, please review it on the site you purchased it. I have no marketing department or marketing budget, so am dependent on satisfied readers to help in publicising the book.

Very best wishes,

Ian Douglas

Readers May Also Be Interested In:

Exploring History in the Scottish Borders", by Ian Douglas,

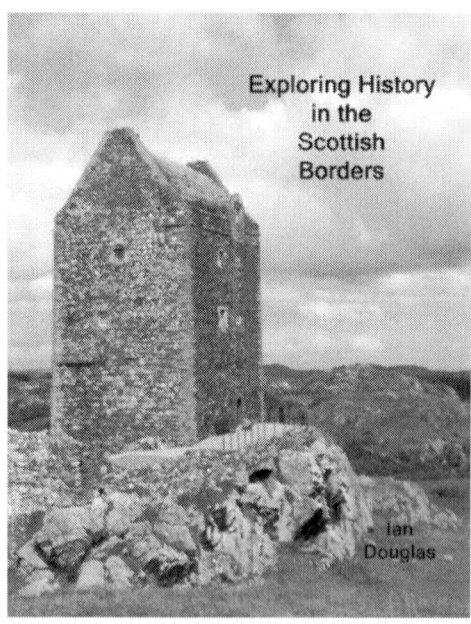

The Scottish border is steeped in history. "**Exploring History in the Scottish Borders**", by Ian Douglas, describes the history of this turbulent area.

The borderland was the crossroads between the north and south of Britain. The often fraught relationship between England and Scotland left its mark on the area and the people. This book tells the story of the English/Scottish borderland from the time of the Romans, through the Scottish wars of independence, the turbulent 16th century and Henry VIII's "rough wooing", up until the reopening of part of the Waverley Line by Queen Elizabeth in 2015.

Illustrated by many full colour photographs, Exploring

History in the Scottish Borders provides an overview of Border history, and a guide to key historical sites in the borderland.

Scotland's Great Lowland Castles – Stirling, Edinburgh, Linlithgow, Doune and St Andrews, by Ian Douglas.

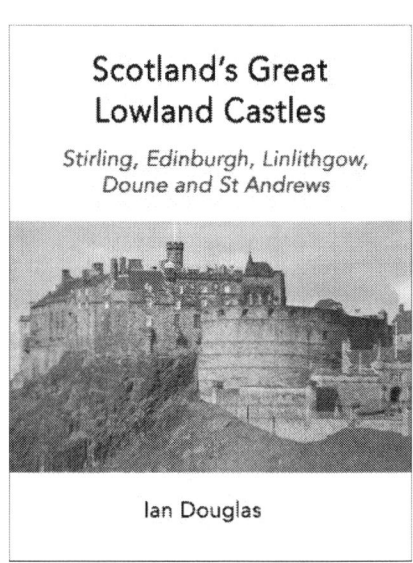

Castles can help bring history to life. The great castles are a tangible link to the past and have a story to tell. This book describes Historic Scotland's five most visited lowland castles, Edinburgh, Stirling, Doune, St Andrews and Linlithgow. As well as providing an armchair tour of the castle it describes their place in Scotland's often turbulent and sometimes heroic history.

If you are considering visiting these great castles, or are just interested in Scotland's history, this book has been written for you.

And a true story from the Second World War

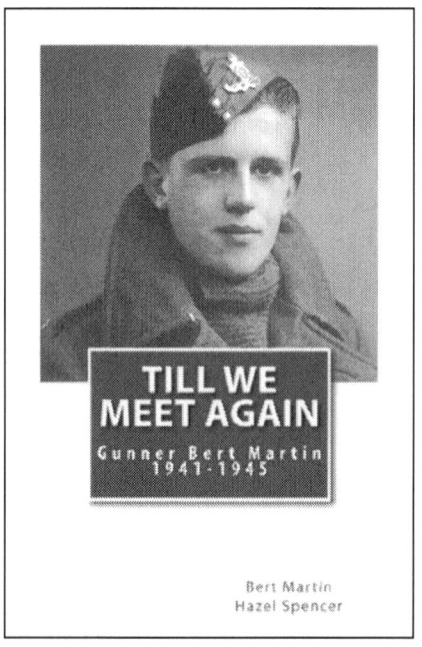

Till We Meet Again: Gunner Bert Martin 1941-1945, by Bert Martin and Hazel Spencer (Bert's daughter who edited his diaries).

Bert was captured at the fall of Tobruk, and his diaries provide an insight into life in a PoW camp, the fears, the boredom, the hunger and the comradeship.

Bert and his comrades were moved from camp to camp as the Nazis retreated. They finally gained their freedom outside Dresden as the war neared its end and made their way through the chaos of a disintegrating Germany to the Allied lines. Now, more than 70 years after Bert wrote his diaries, the story can be told.

This isn't the "Great Escape", it is the true story of an ordinary soldier living through extraordinary times.

Printed in Great Britain
by Amazon